Beverly Hills
with love

Paintings
and Text by

Dorothy
Rice

GLEN HOUSE COMMUNICATIONS

BEVERLY HILLS FROM ABOVE

The view of Beverly Hills from the top of the City Hall tower provides a clear idea behind the notion of the "Golden Triangle," a three-sided segment of the Beverly Hills community that comprises some of the most sought-after, prestigeous and lucrative real estate in the entire world.

The portion of Wilshire Boulevard that runs between Santa Monica Boulevard and Rexford forms the "base" of the Golden Triangle, while Santa Monica Boulevard and Rexford Drive comprise the remaining two sides intersecting to form the "apex" of the triangle.

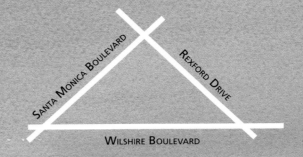

For my husband,
Stanley Chase,
with all my love

Contents

9 MAP OF BEVERLY HILLS

10 THE BIRTH OF A LEGEND

14 ON SUNSET BOULEVARD

30 ON SANTA MONICA BOULEVARD

42 ON WILSHIRE BOULEVARD

62 ON RODEO DRIVE

82 ON NORTH BEVERLY DRIVE

88 ON CAÑON DRIVE

102 LOOKING YOUR BEST IN BEVERLY HILLS

106 ON "LITTLE" SANTA MONICA BOULEVARD

118 ON CAMDEN, BEDFORD, ROXBURY, BRIGHTON AND THE REST

124 ON SOUTH BEVERLY DRIVE

128 LIFE SOUTH OF WILSHIRE

136 LIFE SOUTH OF SUNSET

144 THE EAST END

156 THE ENTERTAINMENT INDUSTRY

174 ABOUT DOROTHY RICE

Acknowledgments

My thanks to:

Stanley Chase for his encouragement and dedication to making this book a reality;

Dana Levy for the book and jacket design;

Scott Huver, editor and researcher;

Editorial consultants Florie Brizel and Mia Kaczinski Dunn;

Beverly Hills Chamber of Commerce and Beverly Hills Visitors Bureau;

Martin Barab, Holly Barnhill, Joseph Broussard, Les Bronte, Gigi Carlton, Robin Chancellor, Donna and Henry Colman, Abe Frank, Grenna Friedman, Darlene Hamilton, Carol Dudley Katzka, Rosalie Lurie, Annie McAuley, Wendy Pratt, Errol Rappaport, Cynthia Savage, Parool K. Shah, Kelly Bevan Spirer, Tom Voltin, Eric Weston and Harriet and Irving White;

The City of Beverly Hills and, of course, the many people, places, sights and sounds that make up this very special community.

Movie star dolls courtesy of the Franklin Mint on Rodeo Drive.

Library of Congress Catalog-in-Publication Data

Rice, Dorothy.
    Beverly Hills with love : paintings and text / by Dorothy Rice. — 1st ed.
      p. cm.
    Includes index.
    ISBN 0-918269-03-2 (hardcover)   Printed In Hong Kong
    1. Rice, Dorothy—Themes, motives. 2. Beverly Hills (Calif.)—In art. 3. Beverly
Hills (Calif.)—Description and travel. I. Title.
ND1839.R48A4 1998
759. 13—dc21   97-34564
                                          CIP

GLEN HOUSE COMMUNICATIONS

P.O. BOX 3663, BEVERLY HILLS, CA 90212-0666

(310) 475-4236 FAX (310) 474-5720

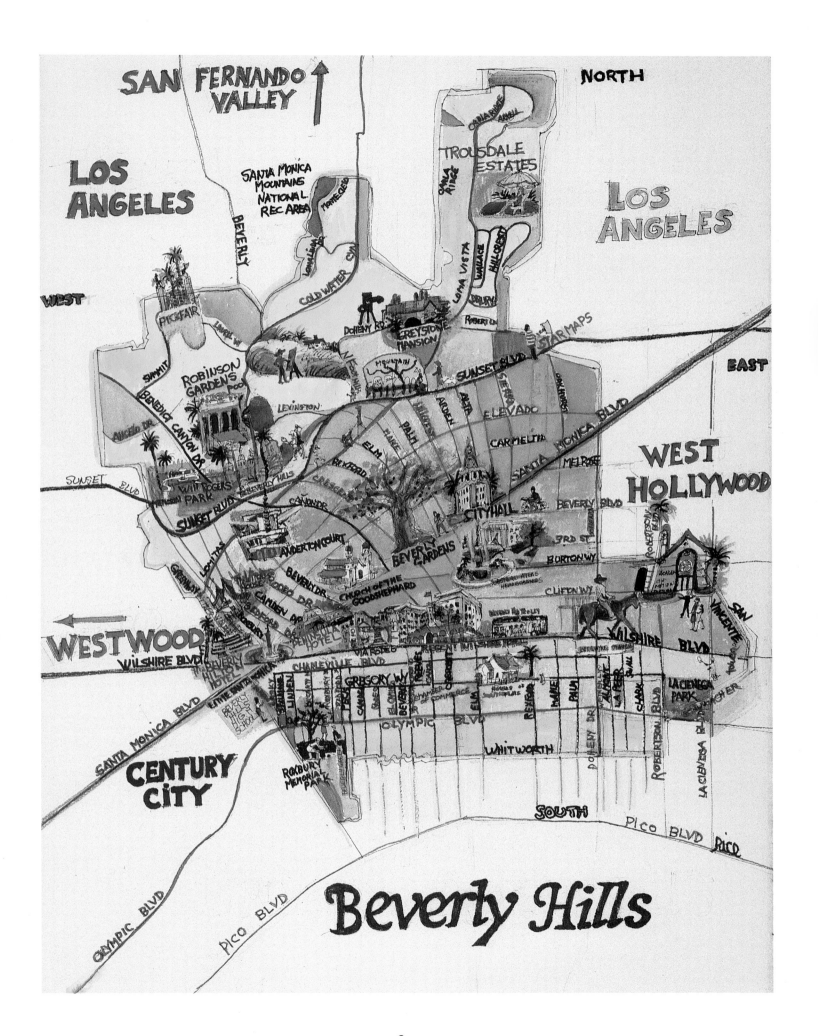

THE BIRTH OF A LEGEND

By the 1890s, California was undergoing a major land boom, and in 1906, a group of oilmen had bought the land that now is Beverly Hills—once a Mexican ranchero. Burton Green christened the city-to-be "Beverly Hills," having been inspired by a newspaper article on President William Taft's visit to Green's hometown, Beverly Farms, Massachusetts (Mrs. Green added the *Hills* in honor of the local topography).

The grand, pink Beverly Hills Hotel was conceived and built in 1911 as a glamorous lure, drawing enough settlers to establish an official city in 1914. One early convert was the famous star of the new motion picture industry Douglas Fairbanks, whose Pickfair mansion became so popular—the city's honorary mayor Will Rogers once proclaimed his only official duty was directing the tourists to Doug and Mary Pickford's place—it

inspired dozens of equally familiar names to move to Beverly Hills, firmly establishing it then, now and forever as the home to the rich and famous.

Today, the city enjoys an emerging new dimension as home not just to entertainment industry stars and moguls, but to many top businesses as well. It has evolved as a wonderful place to live, work and play.

THE GREEN HOME ON PARK WAY
Burton Green, who envisioned the Beverly Hills Hotel, built this three-story 6,500-square-foot English Tudor-style marvel behind Beverly Gardens Park as a home for his daughter in 1907. The second oldest home still standing in the city can be seen from Santa Monica Boulevard.

PICKFAIR >
No single estate can claim to have influenced the development of Beverly Hills as significantly as Pickfair, the legendary hillside home of Douglas Fairbanks and Mary Pickford that inspired a generation of Hollywood superstars to set up housekeeping in Beverly Hills and was soon as well-known in America as the White House.

ROBINSON GARDEN POOL AND PAVILION

Virginia Robinson never missed giving a weekly card party for her close friends in her magnificent pool pavilion, designed in Renaissance style and featuring graffito ornamentation on its exterior, which is contrasted with a Moorish-inspired ceiling and Indian lamps. Virginia was renowned for the spectacular parties—informal teas to black tie extravaganzas—that she threw every week. Many of her soirees took place outdoors and were often completely designed and themed—down to the napkins—around the dress she planned to wear to the party.

THE ROBINSON HOME

This one-story beaux arts-style home offers picture perfect views of the expansive gardens from every window. Virginia Robinson remained an energetic tennis player through age 85. When not tending her gardens, she played on her private tennis court, with her pet monkeys housed in roomy cages set along the width of the court, as her audience. After her husband Harry's early death in 1932, she opened J.W. Robinson outlets in Beverly Hills and Palm Springs and attended every board meeting until her death in 1977, just a few days short of her 100th birthday.

STONE LIONS

I was captivated by the two stone lions, one laughing and one frowning, that watch over the estate, giving me the feeling of being in an enchanted garden.

< VIRGINIA ROBINSON GARDENS

Virginia Robinson set the tone for the stylish lifestyle of early Beverly Hills, and her unflagging energy and exquisite personal taste still endure at her beautiful Elden Way home. The estate, its six terraced gardens, sparkling swimming pool, sizable tennis courts and the overall color scheme she devised reflect the enthusiasm with which she lived her life. Her father, architect Nathaniel Dryden, designed the estate, which was built in 1911 on six sloping acres over a former lima bean field in what soon would become Beverly Hills.

Along the lush trails of exotic flora, cypress trees, sego palms, ear pod trees, monkey hand trees, hibiscus, gardenia trees and many tropical plants first laid out by landscaper Charles Gibbs Adams, a winding series of six intimate Italian terrace gardens—linked by brick pathways and an intricate irrigation system including pools and fountains—cascade through citrus and camellia groves. Over the estate's long lifespan, the assorted palms have grown into a towering two and a half acre tropical forest.

On Jan. 1, 1993 the grounds, which are listed in the National Register of Historic Places, became a privately-run, non-profit institution overseen by The Friends of Robinson Gardens.

ON SUNSET BOULEVARD

If you enter Beverly Hills on Sunset Boulevard from the eastern border and drive toward the Pacific Ocean at the right time of day, there's certainly a chance that you'll witness a gorgeous California sunset.

Beverly Hills put Sunset Boulevard on the map, and the rest of West Los Angeles sprung up around it. Following it from Hollywood to the west, it will lead you through such tony enclaves as Bel-Air, Holmby Hills, Brentwood and Pacific Palisades until it ends at the Pacific Ocean.

But it is in Beverly Hills that Sunset Boulevard best lives up to its legend for hosting the grandest, most opulent and architecturally diverse showplace estates in the world, dividing the *very, very expensive* homes to the immediate south of Sunset from the _really_ *very, very expensive* homes to the immediate north. If you want a glimpse of how the rich and famous live on the West Coast, just jump in your car and follow the sunset on Sunset.

HALLOWEEN ON SUNSET
Much-traveled Sunset Boulevard offers a convenient holiday showplace for the creative talents of this estate home's owner, a principal in the Conroy's flower shop chain. Halloween inspired this spooky theme, just one in a series of elaborate, fun holiday displays that appear at the corner of Sunset Boulevard and Mountain Drive each year.

WILL ROGERS PARK

Yes, the park was named after *that* Will Rogers, the homespun humorist who never met a man he didn't like and made his home in Beverly Hills.

In gratitude for all he had done for Beverly Hills' reputation, the city named a park on Sunset Boulevard across from the Beverly Hills Hotel (designed by the hotel's architect Elmer Grey in 1915) in Rogers' honor in 1952. It was the site of his 1926 "election" as honorary mayor. A popular site for Sunday picnics and leisurely strolls, the park recently underwent a major facelift, which included the upgrade of the 85-year-old fountain and expansive koi pond that serves as its centerpiece, and the installation of a bas-relief plaque recognizing Rogers' role as Beverly Hills' most enthusiastic cheerleader.

THE BEVERLY HILLS HOTEL

Some people say there wouldn't be the Beverly Hills we know today without the venerable "Pink Palace," the Beverly Hills Hotel and Bungalows.

In 1912 the extravagant Beverly Hills Hotel and Bungalows—"the Wonder of the Southland," built at a then-staggering cost of $500,000—opened its doors to the public. As the hotel's cachet grew so did the community around it, and by 1914 the city became officially incorporated.

The showplace became a posh retreat for the rich and famous and inspired the elite to settle here, and for many years the hotel was the city's jewel in the crown.

The Beverly Hills Hotel was closed in 1992 for a massive multimillion-dollar facelift to restore its fading elegance. The hotel, which now seems like a magical portal into a glamorous bygone time, reopened June 3, 1995.

POLO LOUNGE PATIO

In the 1940s The El Jardin restaurant was officially rechristened the Polo Lounge in honor of players and frequent guests Will Rogers, Spencer Tracy, Daryl Zanuck, Tommy Hitchcock and Charlie Wrightsman. Today it remains one of "the" places to see and be seen in, as you enjoy a leisurely lunch shaded by a Brazilian pepper tree.

BEVERLY HILLS HOTEL BUNGALOWS

Favored as a home away from home when I first visited Beverly Hills, the bungalows have shielded many secrets. Eccentric billionaire Howard Hughes stayed in Bungalow 4 off and on for almost 30 years. Marilyn Monroe had a discreet love affair with French film idol Yves Montand in Bungalow 5 (the only one with its own pool) in the 60s. Bungalow 3 hosted Robert Kennedy's family, and it was here they learned of his assassination. John Lennon and Yoko Ono hid for a week in Bungalow 11, a favorite of Marlene Dietrich's. Orson Welles toiled on several never-completed projects in Bungalow 14, and Elizabeth Taylor, whose father, Francis, owned an art gallery within the hotel, lived part time in several of the bungalows with six of her eight (thus far) husbands. If only these walls could talk!

THE POOL AT THE PINK PALACE
You'll never know who you'll spot sunning themselves alongside the pool—where Katharine Hepburn once jumped in fully clothed after a tennis match—or leafing through a magazine in the shade of the cabanas—where Faye Dunaway lounged at dawn in a robe with her Oscar the day after she was named Best Actress for "Network."

GREYSTONE MANSION

This wine-tasting event and silent auction, held by the Beverly Hills Bar Association to benefit indigent families needing legal services, livened up the grounds of Greystone Mansion, one of the most prominent estates in the city and a public park since 1965. Greystone's moody slate-gray Indiana limestone facade, imposing neoclassic stylings and mysterious atmosphere create a quintessential air of California Gothic, but it is also surrounded by some of the loveliest gardens, most beautiful fountains and picturesque stone staircases you can imagine.

The estate was designed by Gordon Kaufmann and built in 1927 by oil tycoon Edward Doheny. Aside from serving as a flamboyant party place, photo shoot or popular location site for films such as "The Bodyguard" and "Batman and Robin," the mansion itself sits silently as a reminder of a bygone time.

MARGIE AND BOB PETERSEN

Margie and Robert Petersen met me in the patio garden of their beautiful Georgian Colonial estate, designed by architect Paul Williams. Bob, a former studio photographer for MGM, is the founder and chairman emeritus of the Petersen Publishing Company, which he started over 40 years ago. Today it is the country's leading publisher of special-interest consumer magazines and books, including *Hot Rod*, *Teen* and *Motor Trend*. He also owns the Petersen Aviation

Company. The lovely Margie is a former top professional model and onetime Miss Rheingold.

The Petersens have made significant contributions to the region's cultural profile—particularly with the establishment of the Petersen Automotive Museum. They have been honored numerous times for their tireless charitable efforts. And, as I discovered when I visited them, their accomplishments are balanced by their warmth, charm and hospitality.

TEA AT THE FORMER HOME OF MARION DAVIES

I was invited to the onetime home of actress Marion Davies, built for her in 1927 by her paramour, publishing tycoon William Randolph Hearst. Aleen Leslie—the wife of showbiz attorney Jacques Leslie and writer of the popular radio show "A Date With Judy," which later became a TV series and then a film starring Jane Powell and Elizabeth Taylor—currently owns the home and has lived there for 35 years. We were joined by her friend Shirley Palmer Collier, a former actress ("The Magic Flame") and later a literary agent for many prominent writers—including her husband, John Collier. Shirley sold Frank Capra the story for "It's a Wonderful Life." Together, they reminisced with me over tea. Today, the only remaining original feature from Davies' era is the multiplicity of mirrors that adorned the bathroom so she could view herself from every angle.

HOUSES ON STILTS

DIANE GLAZER INTERVIEWS ITAMAR RABINOVICH

Diane Glazer, an active board member of the Los Angeles World Affairs Council and former attorney for Columbia Pictures, conducts a cable interview in her and husband Guilford Glazer's spectacular modern home with former Israeli Ambassador Itamar Rabinovich, who headed Israel's peace negotiations with Syria. Rabinovich was the founding director of the Moshe Dayan Center at Tel Aviv University in Israel.

For her notable cable TV series, Diane has interviewed more than 450 world leaders, including Henry Kissinger, Al Gore, George Shultz, James Baker, Jeanne Kirkpatrick, Yitzhak Rabin and Bibi Netanyahu.

POOLSIDE ABOVE THE HILLS

From the ornate pool of her John Wolfe-designed home, Deborah Brener enjoys an unparalleled view of the many estates set against the lush green slopes and canyons of Beverly Hills.

THE HILLS OF BEVERLY >

A HOUSE OF ART IN THE HILLS
I fell in love with this spectacular hillside home, masterfully decorated with beautiful English antiques and some of the most vibrant, colorful and expressive artwork you can imagine. The home's gorgeous pool area, lush gardens and magnificent natural light enhance the overall effect created by the exquisite taste of its owner, art consultant Barbara De Vorzon.

< FELIX, THE BEVERLY HILLS CAT
Meet Felix, an apple-cheeked Siamese cat who has the run of his lavish Beverly Hills estate from dawn to dusk, typically keeping a sharp eye on the bird fluttering on the flower pot above him. Felix generously allows Peter Bart, editor-in-chief of *Variety*, and his wife, Leslie, a prominent ghost writer, to cater to his every need.

THE CAROLE LOMBARD -
CLARK GABLE LOVENEST

Public relations whiz, talent manager and television producer ("Mike Hammer") Jay Bernstein relaxes amidst his collections of theatrical momentos and African safari icons in the living room that once belonged to film legend Carole Lombard back when she was first courted by future husband Clark Gable. Jay came to Hollywood from his native Oklahoma City on a quest to meet his idol, Alan Ladd, and never left, staying on to steer the rise of several star careers, including those of Suzanne Somers, Peter Fonda and Farrah Fawcett—who created the black onyx torso that graces his living room table. He still has stars in his eyes.

KEEPING UP WITH THE JONESES
Where else can you see two side-by-side
multimillion-dollar cliffside mansions with
matching overhanging tennis courts? Watch
out for falling tennis balls!

ELAINE YOUNG ON ARKELL DRIVE
In the competitive, big-money market of
Beverly Hills, real estate agents have been
known to develop personas, mystiques and
publicity equal to the Hollywood stars they
frequently serve, but—after profiles in
magazines like *Time* and *People* during the
boom time of the 1980s—few are as well-
known as Elaine Young, who has made many
sales of magnificent multimillion-dollar
estates to a celebrity clientele.

In contrast to her major professional
stature, the very petite Elaine was dwarfed
by this huge six-bedroom, six-bathroom
estate on scenic Arkell Drive—complete with
an indoor pool and Jacuzzi, and several
ornate and detailed hand-painted ceiling
murals—which she had just shown off to
visiting Middle Eastern royalty.

On "Big" Santa Monica Boulevard

North Santa Monica Boulevard is a major thoroughfare that links its namesake city-by-the sea to the rest of Los Angeles.

Today, traveling east from Century City, past the Beverly Hilton Hotel and across Wilshire Boulevard, Santa Monica Boulevard runs just above the business district of Beverly Hills and just below one of the most desirable residential areas of the city. Most notable along its route are a trio of longstanding churches—All Saints' Episcopal, Beverly Hills Presbyterian and the Church of the Good Shepherd—and the long strip of Beverly Gardens Park, a well kept stretch of greenery that often hosts art shows.

Clearly the main landmark along Santa Monica Boulevard is the splendorous Civic Center, home to the seat of city government, the police and fire departments and the public library. Few visitors to Beverly Hills can pass by City Hall without marveling at its architectural majesty. It genuinely looks how you would expect Beverly Hills' city hall to look.

THE ELECTRIC FOUNTAIN
Standing at the much-traveled intersection of Wilshire Boulevard and Santa Monica Boulevard is the Electric Fountain, bathed in a continuous aquatic spray and lit at night by exotic, colored lights. The cast-concrete statue topping the center column is a Native American figure captured in a rain prayer. A bas relief frieze around the fountain's base by sculptor Merrill Gage depicts the history of California. Beneath the fountain is a large underground vault, where Jack Benny used to claim he kept all his money.

ALL SAINTS' EPISCOPAL CHURCH
The luminous interior of All Saints' Episcopal Church is understandably inspiring to its faithful congregation, which has included celebrated leaders and notables from all walks of life since its dedication in 1925.

CITY HALL

THE AFFAIRE IN THE GARDENS
The biannual Affaire in the Gardens is one of the most eagerly awaited events in Beverly Hills. More than 200 artists converge on Beverly Gardens Park to peddle their creations and demonstrate their talents, setting up exhibits to inform and entertain the approximately 50,000 visitors who turn out for the weekend show.

THE CHURCH OF THE GOOD SHEPHERD
The first church to be built in Beverly Hills, the Catholic Church of the Good Shepherd adds classic beauty to Santa Monica Boulevard. The church has captured the attention of the world since 1924: the funeral of Rudolph Valentino and Elizabeth Taylor's first wedding, to Nicky Hilton, were among the services held there.

Rice

TREE IN BEVERLY GARDENS PARK

Two friends enjoy the shade of the massive 65-foot-tall Moreton bay fig tree that is one of the highlights of Beverly Gardens Park. At 80+ years of age, the fig tree is believed to be one of the oldest of its kind in all of California and has a canopy circumference of more than twice its height. Beverly Hills takes its trees very seriously and has been named an official "Tree City, USA," with some proud locals often proclaiming that there are more trees than residents. The city has undertaken three ambitious Street Tree Master Plans, which have lined over 30 of Beverly Hills' most attractive byways with species like the Chinese flame, red ironbark, pink tabebuia, Southern magnolia, and—of course—more than a few varieties of palm trees.

CULTURAL FESTIVAL
One of four professional groups that performed on this Sunday afternoon at the Civic Center Plaza, the AVAZ International Dance Theater of singers and dancers utilize the movements and music of a centuries-rich tradition of Persian culture.

SPANISH DANCERS
Lola Montez and her Spanish Dancers add a Latin flair to the Cultural Festival.

OPPOSITE PAGE
THE BEVERLY HILLS CIVIC CENTER
An architectural gem, the Civic Center is located at the crossroads of Rexford Drive and Santa Monica Boulevard. It is built around the original 1932 William Gage-designed City Hall, at the heart of which remains the tower capped by a colorful dome and guilded cupola.

Stunning from all angles, inside and outside, this extraordinary maze of structures was designed by Charles W. Moore.

THE BEVERLY HILLS PRESBYTERIAN CHURCH

Standing at the corner of Santa Monica Boulevard and Rodeo Drive since 1925, the chimes of the bucolic Presbyterian Church can be heard pealing throughout central Beverly Hills. This was the family church of actor Jimmy Stewart.

THE BEVERLY HILLS PUBLIC LIBRARY

The Beverly Hills Public Library is a magnet not just for local citizens and young students but also for established academics, professional writers and researchers and literature lovers from all over. The library actively reaches out to the community with a never-ending series of literary and cultural presentations, readings, forums and performances designed to appeal to groups of all ages and interests.

LOVE IN THE PALM COURT OF THE CIVIC CENTER >

THE CIVIC CENTER AT NIGHT
The venerable City Hall tower is splashed with light from all sides and stands as an opulent beacon to Beverly Hills.

THE BEVERLY HILLS POLICE DEPARTMENT
The Beverly Hills Police Department has over 130 sworn officers and many civilian members and is among the best trained and equipped police departments in the nation. This BHPD booth at the Affaire in the Gardens, where officers provide safety and crime prevention tips to residents, is part of the force's outreach to the community.

< CIVIC CENTER PLAZA
This space—formerly nicknamed the "Boat Court" due to its ship-like shape—is frequently used for city-sponsored events and receptions. On this day, in conjunction with the Beverly Hills Public Library, dozens of children were celebrating a special Reader's Group created to encourage the joy of reading.

SKATER ON SANTA MONICA BOULEVARD

A DRAMATIC DEMONSTRATION

Dozens of local children and adults *ooohhed* and *aaahhed* as members of the Beverly Hills Fire Department staged an emergency firefighting demonstration, spraying the roof of the public library with water and sliding down this cable from the dizzying heights of an engine ladder as part of Fire Service Day. Families turned out to show their support for BHFD, as well as for a few free hot dogs, a show of the metal-snapping power of the Jaws of Life and a ride through town on a real fire engine.

THE BEVERLY HILLS FIRE DEPARTMENT

The Beverly Hills Fire Department is one of the finest firefighting and emergency rescue operations in the country. The fire station supports a full-time staff of 90, houses BHFD's special vehicles and equipment, and provides a full kitchen and mess hall, exercise center, and administrative offices for the department, its Fire Prevention Center and the CPR training program. At the center is an elaborate training court, where firefighters can practice ladder rescues, tear into scrap vehicles with the Jaws of Life and test new fire suppression technologies.

THE MAYORAL INSTALLATION

I was on hand for the 1997 installation of MeraLee Goldman, in the black-and-yellow ensemble, a onetime professional city planner turned public servant and a prominent advocate of arts and culture. Countless local civic, business and government officials turned out to wish Mayor Goldman well.

Those in the know in Beverly Hills will recognize such insiders as former Mayor Allan Alexander and his wife, Joan; the city's Director of Special Events and Filming, Robin Chancellor; MeraLee's husband, attorney Leonard Goldman; former Mayor Max Salter and his wife, Janet; Fire Chief Clarence Martin; local journalists Mia Kaczinski Dunn and Scott Huver; Councilmember Tom Levyn and his wife, Karen; the city's Director of Public Affairs and Information, Fred Cunningham; Beverly Hills School Board student representative Allison Hoffman; Councilmember Vicki Reynolds and Murray Pepper; and Los Angeles County District Attorney Gil Garcetti.

ON WILSHIRE BOULEVARD

Gaylord Wilshire, one of Los Angeles' most colorful millionaire socialites, was just 35 in the late 1880s when he paid $50,000 in gold coins for a barley field just west of Downtown Los Angeles. He created a roadway 120-feet wide, convinced that Los Angeles would never be one of the world's truly great cities until it had a truly great boulevard, which he naturally named after himself. That pioneering roadway would eventually stretch all the way from Downtown Los Angeles to Beverly Hills and to the Pacific Ocean.

Today, enormous, elaborate and ornate display windows dominate Beverly Hills' "Department Store Row," a corridor of the world's most fashionable retailers, including Neiman-Marcus, Barneys New York, Robinsons-May and *two* wings of Saks Fifth Avenue.

Also lining Wilshire Boulevard are extravagant world-class hotels like the Regent Beverly Wilshire Hotel, the Beverly Hilton Hotel, and the Radisson Beverly Pavilion Hotel. Alongside the hotels are a plethora of internationally known banks and other financial institutions, as well as recent high-profile additions like Planet Hollywood and Niketown, just steps away from tranquil residential areas.

JOHN WAYNE STATUE
Noted Western-themed sculptor Harry Jackson, a good friend of "The Duke's," created this towering, majestic monument to Wayne's mythic frontier image for the Great Western Bank—for which Wayne used to be the commercial spokesman—at La Cienega and Wilshire Boulevards.

EDWARDS-LOWELL FURS
At her elegant designer fur salon, Grace Lowell helps two of her most vivacious customers select their furs for the upcoming season. Sexy Rhonda Shear—the popular comedienne and late-night movie hostess of USA Cable's "Up All Night"—is wrapped in an appropriately sheer beaver coat. Meanwhile, sultry Irina Maleeva—the Bulgarian-born actress from "Fellini Satyricon" who also designed Edwards-Lowell's opulent chandelier—opts for a beguiling chinchilla coat. The newly redesigned salon is a model of classic luxury and brings a fresh element of glamour to its Wilshire Boulevard location.

RADISSON BEVERLY PAVILION HOTEL
Another of Wilshire Boulevard's busy hotels, it prides itself on European-style intimacy, personal attention and a prime location in the heart of the city, as well as Colette, its charming in-house continental restaurant.

REGENT BEVERLY WILSHIRE HOTEL

Inspired by the city's emerging status as a posh tourist destination and playground for Hollywood stars, the luxurious Regent Beverly Wilshire Hotel opened the doors of its magnificent Italian Renaissance/beaux arts structure to guests in 1928 and has been one of the major centerpieces of Beverly Hills hospitality ever since, changing its distinctive, colorful awnings to match the seasons. Situated in one of the most desirable locations in the world, on Wilshire Boulevard at the foot of Rodeo Drive, it brings a touch of classic Old World charm mingled with Southern California airiness to the Golden Triangle.

This landmark hotel was expanded in 1970, with the addition of a new wing, by famed hotelier Hernando Courtright, who recommended me to the Los Angeles Southwest Museum for my first museum show, of Mexican oil paintings. Three of the world's great fashion names are located off the lobby: Escada, Buccellati and Avi. A brick walkway crosses Wilshire Boulevard from the hotel to 2 Rodeo Drive.

The hotel's Presidential Suite is best known to movie lovers as "The Pretty Woman Suite" since much of the popular Richard Gere/Julia Roberts romantic comedy was shot here. Other films shot here include "Clueless," "Indecent Proposal," American Gigolo" and "Beverly Hills Cop."

EL CAMINO REAL
Unmistakable European touches, such as the authentic lanterns from England's Edinburgh Castle, meet traditional Beverly Hills opulence when gleaming limousines and luxury cars drop off guests on the cobblestone entrance of the private inner courtyard of the Regent Beverly Wilshire Hotel as international flags flutter above.

ESCADA
The colorful awnings of the Regent Beverly Wilshire Hotel help its world-class Escada boutique catch the eye of serious shoppers along Wilshire Boulevard. Walk across the street to 2 Rodeo's Escada Sport store for more playful wardrobe choices.

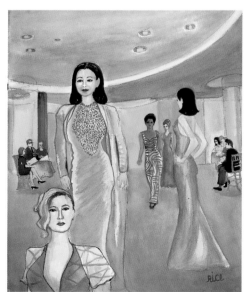

SAKS FIFTH AVENUE FASHION SHOW
Style was the order of the day at the "Signatures of Evening" luncheon and fashion show in Saks Fifth Avenue's Designer Salon, as a procession of gorgeous models displayed the latest in evening wear. Who could choose between Donald Deal's terrific chocolate satin dress with beaded overlay or Marc Bower's striking apple green velour gown and matching coat? Or maybe the sleek, gold cut velvet gown by Christian Lacroix? And then there's that wild velvet zebra jacket and crepe pants by Yves Saint Laurent...I'll take them *all*!

CHRISTMAS AT THE REGENT BEVERLY WILSHIRE HOTEL
During the holidays the Regent Beverly Wilshire Hotel takes on an enchanted air when, illuminated by hundreds of white lights and topped with a stylized Christmas tree, it becomes one of the focal points of Beverly Hills' seasonal celebrations. Each year the holiday shopping season is kicked off by a dramatic lighting ceremony during which the rooftop tree and all of the holiday lights in the Golden Triangle come to life in tandem.

SOTHEBY'S

It was "ladies' night" at Sotheby's glamorous Beverly Hills headquarters as the notable auction house unveiled a collection of enviable icons and artifacts from the estates of first lady of song Ella Fitzgerald and "Road" movie queen Dorothy Lamour. Fitzgerald's shiny, pearl-gray 1960 Mercedes-Benz 300-D Cabriolet fetched a whopping $74,000, her baby grand piano was snared for $7,250 by a New York jazz combo, and even her false eyelashes went for $900. Among the Lamour memorabilia were a fabulous jewelry collection the actress wore in "The Greatest Show on Earth" and, of course, some of the trademarks sarongs that Lamour made famous.

COUNTER SPY SHOP OF LONDON ⊁

Offering a healthy dose of paranoia in the age of industrial espionage, this James Bond-ian boutique offers such options as telephones with built-in lie detectors, anti-theft briefcases that generate electrical shocks by remote control and even full bulletproofing for your car.

NIKETOWN >

Massive Niketown first made its footprint on Wilshire Boulevard in 1996 and has been serving a busy throng of sneaker-loving customers ever since. It is one of the nation's largest retail outlets for athletic footwear, officially licensed apparel and other sporting goods and serves as the chain's Los Angeles area flagship.

SLIPPING INTO STYLE AT SAKS

Entertainment reporter and television personality Katie Wagner gets zipped up in a $15,000 Herve Leger signature original in Saks Fifth Avenue's elegant Designer Salon by costume designer and wardrobe stylist Deborah Rowland Stambul. The fabulous clothes Deborah selected are made even *more* fabulous by Katie, who, as the daughter of actor Robert Wagner and Marian Marshall Wagner, grew up in Beverly Hills and attended every one of the local schools. Warm and direct, Katie confided that she hopes one day to settle down in the flats of Beverly Hills with the man of her dreams.

SAKS FIFTH AVENUE

Built in 1938 from the notable designs of John and Donald Parkinson and Paul R. Williams, the classic Moderne Regency-style Saks Fifth Avenue building has been a West Coast mecca for upscale shoppers from around the globe for the last six decades. In 1995 the store underwent a complete facelift—extending the main level along Wilshire Boulevard for a full block, adding an expanded cosmetics department and installing high-speed escalators—to become the chain's West Coast flagship.

Saks added the neighboring Moderne-style property and created a men's store with added women's specialty sizes. Now with two wings offering everything of quality under the sun, Saks Fifth Avenue continues to be one of Beverly Hills' premier providers of elegance and style.

ART OPENING AT PACE WILDENSTEIN
This Jim Dine exhibition was attended by
notables from the world of art, entertainment
and business, including artist David Hockney,
director Sydney Pollack, producer Stanley Chase
and songwriters Marilyn and Alan Bergman.

BARNEYS DEPARTMENT STORE PARKING LOT
This is the view from the many apartment
buildings and small homes tucked behind
Barneys, where shoppers are attended by
what many consider to be the smoothest valet
parking operation in the Los Angeles area.

OPPOSITE PAGE
BARNEYS' GRAND STAIRCASE
Barneys New York opened the doors of its
grand five-story structure in Beverly Hills in
1994, joining the pantheon of legendary
department stores that dot Wilshire Boulevard.
With its winding centerpiece, the Grand
Staircase, the store serves as host to fabulous
charity events such as the Fire and Ice Ball and
established its top-floor Barney Greengrass the
Sturgeon King restaurant as a lunchtime must.

PLANET HOLLYWOOD

Sylvester Stallone, Arnold Schwarzenegger, Bruce Willis and Demi Moore brought their commercial colossus Planet Hollywood to Beverly Hills in 1995. The restaurant—the chain's first in the Los Angeles area—opened with much fanfare, including a block party on Rodeo Drive attended by virtually every star in Tinseltown and featuring entertainment by Elton John, Chuck Berry and partner Willis. The memorabilia collection includes major Hollywood items such as the original "Stagecoach" from the 1939 film directed by John Ford.

"YOU TARZAN, ME JANE"

I donned my tightest animal print outfit and headed over to Planet Hollywood Beverly Hills with my SAG card in hand to "audition" for the part of Jane, the traditional love interest for the syndicated TV series "Tarzan: The New Adventures." The producers wisely chose this site for the open casting call. The wild zebra-striped patterns of the restaurant made a fitting backdrop for the dozens of lovely, incredibly fit young actresses who filled the booths and studied their lines intensely, each wistfully hoping that this would be their "big break." Remembering my own rounds of harrowing auditions in the past, I wished them *all* good luck.

BEVERLY HILLS INN >
This elegant hide-away hotel featuring a banana palm-shaded pool area greets you at the western edge of Beverly Hills, on South Spalding Drive, just off Wilshire Boulevard. You can awaken to a complimentary full breakfast in bed! Later, enjoy a relaxing afternoon tea, complete with fruit and cheese, in the bar lounge.

HARD CANDY AT NEIMAN MARCUS

Dineh Mohajer, the young and effusive founder of the
Funky Color Cosmetic Company, chats it up with the TV
crew from the London-based morning show "The Big
Breakfast" during an interview at Neiman Marcus. After
only a year and a half in the cosmetics industry, Dineh
struck gold—and dozens of other colors—with her trend-
setting, mega-popular Hard Candy line of nail polish.
When I met her, she was particularly excited about her
"Candyman" nail polish, designed especially for men.

THE ESTÉE LAUDER SPA

I underwent a fantastic European aromaspa lymphatic
leg therapy from Mimi at the state-of-the-art Estée
Lauder Spa on the lower level of Neiman Marcus Beverly
Hills. The spa truly pampers its guests with attentive
service and the most advanced techniques available.

NEIMAN MARCUS

A longtime favorite of Beverly Hills' shoppers, the bulk of whom take their consumer-spending duties to heart, Neiman Marcus caters to the finest tastes with an extensive collection of fashions, furs, jewels and unique gifts outlined in the department store's annual "wish list" catalogue. Can't make up your mind? That's okay; Neiman's can provide you with your own personal shopper to help you make the perfect decision.

THE BEVERLY HILTON

Thousands of contestants have walked away as big winners from Merv Griffin's popular syndicated game shows "Wheel of Fortune" and "Jeopardy," but Merv himself may be the biggest winner of all, as the success of his entertainment empire has allowed him to become the top man behind The Beverly Hilton Hotel, one of the principal hospitality venues in the city.

The hotel's International Ballroom remains a popular site in the area for some of the most important rituals of the entertainment industry, such as the American Film Institute's Lifetime Achievement Award, the American Cinema Awards and particularly the annual Golden Globe Awards. Each January the gala, thrown by the Beverly Hills-based Hollywood Foreign Press Association, draws all of the leading luminaries in film, television and music for a night of glamour that is the early indicator of the yearly Oscar race.

TRADER VIC'S

A satellite bar and restaurant of the Beverly Hilton Hotel, Trader Vic's features a Polynesian cuisine. It remains one of the city's most enduring watering holes.

FIRST AMERICANS IN THE ARTS AWARDS

The International Ballroom of the Beverly Hilton Hotel was the site for the Fifth Annual Awards recognizing outstanding achievement by Native Americans in the performing arts. Carroll O'Connor was among the guests who paid homage to the award recipients.

BANKS ON WILSHIRE

More than 50 major financial institutions are located within the city limits, effectively making Beverly Hills "the Wall Street of the West." Most of the city's major bank buildings rise along Wilshire Boulevard, including the impressive spires of Imperial Bank, Manufacturers Bank, Home Federal, Wells Fargo, City National Bank, Security Pacific, Union Bank, Bank of America, Century Bank and Great Western. The structures also house financial offices for investment interests from around the globe.

POOLSIDE AT THE BEVERLY HILTON >

Could there be a more tranquil spot for soaking up the Southern California sunshine than poolside at the Beverly Hilton Hotel? As if the warm rays and laid-back ambience aren't enough luxury, just steps away lies Griff's, the casual poolside restaurant.

ON RODEO DRIVE

One of the first three streets laid out in 1911 along with Beverly and Cañon Drives, Rodeo Drive takes its world-famous name from Rancho Rodeo de las Aguas, the Spanish ranchero that originally occupied the area now known as Beverly Hills. Although it has become one of the most legendary shopping streets on the globe, its origins were more humble, as once much of what is Rodeo Drive was a bridle path leading to the Beverly Hills Hotel.

Shops first started springing up on Rodeo Drive in the 1950s to service the city's residents, and the street had the feel of a small town when I first visited Rodeo Drive in the late 1960s, but in the early 1970s several retailers on the street banded together to promote it as an important center of high fashion. The world listened, and soon the three-block stretch of Rodeo Drive between Wilshire and Santa Monica Boulevards became home to dozens of internationally known stores, a veritable "Who's Who" of designer names and the leading tourist destination in the Los Angeles area.

One thing about the street is certain: Unlike so many highly-hyped tourist destinations, with all of its legendary over-the-top glamour, Rodeo Drive *never* fails to live up to a visitor's wildest expectations.

FIRE TRUCK PASSING CHANEL ON RODEO DRIVE

GIORGIO BEVERLY HILLS
With its bright and airy ambience and signature yellow and white decor, Giorgio remains one of the highlights of the Rodeo Drive shopping experience. It actually employs a sophisticated lighting and temperature control system that is designed to approximate the *perfect* sunshiny Southern California day inside, no matter what the weather is outside!

RODEO DRIVE SHOPS >
The ultimate shopper's paradise, the street sparkles as brilliantly as one of the many gems that can be found for sale in its numerous jewelry shops. Whether you travel by limo or on foot, you have a myriad of stores to choose from—including Frances Klein Estate Jewelry, Amphora, Battaglia and Van Cleef & Arpels—where some of the top finery in the world can be found.

VIA RODEO AT 2 RODEO

Here you'll discover many of the world's most legendary stores in a stage-like, open-air setting as you step into a world of architectural contrasts. There are more than 20 major shops, boutiques and restaurants, including Tiffany & Co., Escada Sport, Cartier, Christian Dior, José Eber, Valentino, Sulka, Porsche Design, McCormick & Schmick's, Jessica McClintock, Gianfranco Ferre and Ginza Sushiko, the most exclusive sushi place anywhere.

The concourse is practically a mini-theme park with its own faux-cobblestone walking street and a small-scale replica of Rome's Spanish Steps. 2 Rodeo is a photo-op dream.

BVLGARI

The innovative yet classic design of Bvlgari, ideally situated at the ultra-prominent intersection of Wilshire Boulevard and Rodeo Drive, imparts a unique and international flavor to that corner. Inside is a vast array of magical merchandise, which includes some of the most beautiful, highly-sought-after Italian jewelry in the world. Somehow, Bvlgari manages to capture and refine everyone's fantasy vision of fine gems and accessories in its to-die-for designs.

PARKING AT 2 RODEO

This very sophisticated and elegant-looking valet service nestled under the lavish 2 Rodeo complex is one of the best bargains in town, offering two free hours of parking! In fact, the city has invested major amounts of money into developing over a dozen parking lots that offer lengthy free parking in a safe, clean environment.

THE CAT'S MEOW AT HARRY WINSTON
Beauty authority and author Beverly Sassoon
outfits her feline friend Philly in the
trademark finery of the renowned jeweler
Harry Winston on Rodeo Drive. Harry Winston
has been dazzling the world since 1932,
adorning generations of stars and socialites
with sumptuous diamonds, rubies, emeralds,
sapphires and pearls—including the famed
Hope Diamond and the Taylor-Burton
engagement ring. Beverly, a former actress, is
taking her beauty expertise to a whole new
clientele, developing a high-end grooming
product line for cats and dogs.

TOMMY HILFIGER

"Tommy World" is ultra-hip, über-popular designer Tommy Hilfiger's half-joking nickname for his two-story, 20,000-square-foot flagship retail complex on Rodeo Drive. A veritable mini-department store loaded with Hilfiger's bold signature stylings—from shirts to shoes to athletic gear—the complex also features a golf shop, an array of leather goods, an espresso bar, a Wolfgang Puck cafe, a high tech sound system, an exclusive "Rock 'n' Roll" line of clothing available only in the Beverly Hills store and, perhaps most importantly, VIP service for Hilfiger's many celebrity customers. Those customers range from Snoop Doggy Dogg to Sheryl Crow, from Hugh Grant to No Doubt, and from Bjork to Bill Clinton.

MEETING FRIENDS AT VIA RODEO

McCORMICK & SCHMICK'S
A pair of sprightly swordfish-shaped topiaries greets you at the entrance to McCormick & Schmick's The Fish House, the popular seafood restaurant on Via Rodeo. The paneled eatery offers an array of ocean-derived dishes, a sunny outdoor patio perfect for people-watching and a side bar with a sign that counts down the days to St. Patrick's Day.

CAROLERS AT 2 RODEO

TIFFANY & CO.

Rodeo Drive regulars eagerly await each new window display from Tiffany & Co., including this splendid Christmas creation. With entries on both Via Rodeo and Rodeo Drive, Tiffany & Co. serves as the anchor store for the Euro-styled 2 Rodeo complex and hosts "Breakfast at Tiffany's" special events, including one which featured at least a half-dozen Audrey Hepburn look-alikes modeling jewelry.

PRESTIGIOUS SHOPS
AT RODEO AND WILSHIRE

Where else in the world will you find shops like Valentino, Christian Dior, Cartier and Tiffany & Co. just steps away from each other, with Bvlgari right across the street? Only at this famed intersection in Beverly Hills.

LALIQUE

The inimitable Lalique look sparkes throughout the store from the smallest gleaming cameo pins and brooches to a dining table made completely of translucent crystal. The theme even carries out onto the store's façade, where several crystalline faces beam at you.

HOLIDAY TIME IN BEVERLY HILLS
Sipping cappuccino to the holiday sounds of carolers at Piazza Rodeo in the 2 Rodeo complex amidst the beribboned and holly-adorned lamp posts and a classically styled Christmas tree.

BARBIE ON RODEO DRIVE

The famous street was all dolled up for the
holidays when the Rodeo Drive Committee
called in Barbie, the fashionable icon of little
girls everywhere, for its annual celebration.
The street was paved with pink carpet, there
was an ongoing fashion show of Barbie
couture through the years with live models,
a Barbie "museum" and an auction of dolls
decked out and accessorized by some of
Rodeo Drive's top designers and shops, all
to benefits AIDS charities for children.

BARBIE'S WHEELS

As seen on display in Louis Vuitton's window,
this Barbie doll obviously traded in her Malibu
dream house for this sweet Beverly Hills ride,
a pink car laden with Louis Vuitton baggage,
totes and suitcases from the chic luggage shop.

THE COLBERT FESTIVAL

The Colbert Foundation, dedicated to promoting goodwill between America and France, appropriately chose internationally famed Rodeo Drive in Beverly Hills (the sister city of Cannes, France) for its "La Journée Des Artisans" event, a living exhibition of French craftsmanship. Among the many luxury items were specially hand crafted "Objets Extraordinaire" inspired and autographed by Martin Scorsese, Sharon Stone, Angelica Huston and Jaclyn Smith, which were all auctioned off for charity.

THE YELLOW ROLLS ROYCE

This gorgeous Rolls Royce owned by Fred Hayman is often seen parked on Rodeo Drive.

ANDERTON COURT

This building on North Rodeo Drive, designed by Frank Lloyd Wright in 1953 in a streamlined, nautical Moderne Style, is the only building of Wright's in Beverly Hills. It represents one of his zanier creations with its zigzagged ramp and jagged spire. Shops line the ramp around a rising metal mast. Avi Men's Wear, Tallarico, Fernando Romero Salon, Kazanjiian and Fogarty and Holiday Express Travel currently occupy the building.

GUCCI

International travelers of every persuasion find the allure of Gucci irresistible. One of the most renowned names on Rodeo Drive, Gucci is credited with helping establish the street as the number one fashion center in the world.

SUMMIT HOTEL

This boutique hotel stands right in the midst of bustling Rodeo Drive. It is probably best known for its street-level terrace restaurant, Cafe Rodeo, where diners can feel like movie stars as the hundreds of passers-by peer into the open-air enclosure hoping for a glimpse of someone famous.

THE PHOTO SHOOT

FERRARI FUN ON RODEO DRIVE

The street in front of the Theodore boutique—one of the earliest clothiers on Rodeo Drive—was awash in a sea of red, yellow and black Italian sportscars in 1997 when the legendary automaker Ferrari brought more than 160 models from its classic supercharged line to Rodeo Drive to create the "Concourse D'Elegance" and celebrate 50 years of automotive excellence. Piero Ferrari himself led the event and unveiled the company's new V-12-powered 550 Maranello, the 485-horsepower successor to the venerable Testarosa.

< MOSCHINO WINDOW

With a playful sense of humor and an avant-garde approach to design, Moschino's window displays are always among the most striking—and amusing—on Rodeo Drive.

CROSSWALK ON RODEO DRIVE AND BRIGHTON WAY

You never know who you will catch in the crosswalks of Beverly Hills. On this particular afternoon, Hollywood's highest paid screenwriter, Joe Eszterhas—who penned "Basic Instinct," "Fatal Attraction" and "An Alan Smithee Film-Burn Hollywood Burn"—caught my eye.

DAVID ORGELL
Diamonds are, of course, forever, and at the rate that it's going, jewelry boutique David Orgell just might be, too. Open for more than 40 years, this little gem of a shop is the oldest jewelry and gift retailer on Rodeo Drive.

CARTIER
One of the major gems in the crown of Rodeo Drive, the famed international jeweler Cartier stands as one of the best retailers of timelessly elegant adornments in Beverly Hills.

OPPOSITE PAGE
LOOKING SHARP AT BIJAN
Handsome actor Boyd Holister, who made a name for himself playing actor Clark Gable opposite Cheryl Ladd in the TV movie "The Grace Kelly Story" and again in a one-man stage show, descends the sweeping staircase of the Bijan boutique on Rodeo Drive. He is bearded for a new role and is decked out in some of the designer's trademark finery: a $3,500 blue tropical weight wool sports jacket accentuated by a signature yellow limited-edition (one of four) necktie and pochette. Known for his "by appointment only" policy and provocative ad campaigns featuring celebrities like Bo Derek and Michael Jordan, Bijan has enjoyed 25 years of great success in Beverly Hills.

INSIDE THE RODEO COLLECTION
The unique Rodeo Collection, which houses a number of stylish boutiques, has been a part of Rodeo Drive since 1980. The shopping center is a glossy and fashionable fixture on the fabled street.

**MONDI FASHION SHOW
AT THE RODEO COLLECTION**
Among the Beverly Hills high-fashion crowd at this press opening sponsored by *Vogue* were movie dancer icon Ann Miller and actress Suzanne Somers.

FRENCH STYLE ON RODEO DRIVE

Does this shop look familiar? It was the Rodeo Drive boutique owned by the title characters in the motion picture "Romy and Michelle's High School Reunion," who enjoyed folding scarves there after realizing their long-sought-after dreams. But don't go in expecting to find Lisa Kudrow or Mira Sorvino behind the sales counter. Instead, you might see hot young actresses browsing through various selections from Gucci, which decided to step into the site during a remodeling job on the original Gucci boutique down the street.

THE RODEO COLLECTION

Tall, modern, pink marble arches and oversized round windows face Rodeo Drive. Within, designer boutiques such as Bijan, Gianni Versace, Mondi and Fila are arranged around a sunken courtyard. Built in 1981 by Daryoush Mahboubi-Fardi, the architect was Oliver Vidal.

ON NORTH BEVERLY DRIVE

Beverly Drive was the city's first true center of commerce, hosting many of the earliest shops in Beverly Hills. In recent years, the stretch above Wilshire Boulevard has taken on a new role as a prime location for many nationally known stores that have positioned themselves just one street away from the ritz and glitz of Rodeo Drive.

Victoria's Secret, Blockbuster Music, Banana Republic, The Gap and Williams-Sonoma in the fabulous clock tower parking structure are just some of the familiar names that line Beverly Drive today. They fit in alongside local institutions like Geary's and new landmarks like the glamorous Museum of Television & Radio, which anchors the street to the north.

The street is bolstered by local restaurants like Nate 'N Al's, Louise's, The Cheesecake Factory, Il Fornaio, Jacopo's, R.J.'s The Rib Joint and unique new eateries like Wolfgang Puck's ObaChine.

CLOCK TOWER AND PARKING STRUCTURE
Like a magnet, this newly constructed building on North Beverly Drive entices you to enter the portals of its charming Southwest design. With its landmark clock tower, you can time your two hours of free parking in this large city-owned lot from almost anywhere in the Golden Triangle.

Dedicated in 1996, the building also houses Williams-Sonoma, its spacious interior filled to the ceiling with an overwhelming collection of the finest in cookware and kitchen accessories.

EDWARD KATZKA AT IL FORNAIO

In Beverly Hills, you'll frequently encounter people who, with some luck, talent and dedication, just might be tomorrow's top names in the entertainment industry. I had lunch with one aspiring "player" at Il Fornaio, the sumptuous Italian bakery/restaurant on Beverly Drive which has become a hip meeting place for young up-and-comers—Edward Katzka, the son of the late, much-beloved producer Gabe Katzka and his wife, Carol Dudley Katzka.

CLASSIC WHEELS AT GEARY'S

I spotted this classic 1934 Packard Phaeton parked outside Geary's one Sunday afternoon and wondered if it belonged to the store's owner, Bruce Meyer, a dyed-in-the-wool automotive enthusiast who keeps a jumpsuit once owned by Evel Knievel in his office. I later found out that the the car was indeed Bruce's, of course.

< GEARY'S

Operating on Beverly Drive since the 1930s and the recent recipient of a magical architectural facelift, Geary's—with its sweeping mezzanine, grand stairway and wrought-iron railings—is *the* treasure trove to go to in Beverly Hills for that special gift when your wife just made partner in the firm, your favorite bride-and-groom-to-be just got registered or your best client just won an Emmy. Stocked with a glittering array of chic home accessories, bric-a-brac and tabletop furnishings, the only vexing problem Geary's poses is deciding exactly *which* items of its great miscellanea you will walk out with.

ISRAELI DISCOUNT BANK

This distinctive Moorish-style building designed by L.A. Smith stands out with its onion-shaped dome. It began its existence in 1925 as the Beverly Theater, site of countless fabulous movie premieres in the 30s and 40s. Later it became the Israeli Discount Bank. Santa and his reindeer traditionally swoop over Wilshire Boulevard every Christmas season, but when Mr. Claus and company were briefly "retired" in 1996, the public outcry was so severe that a shiny new sleigh was obtained and installed just before December 25th rolled around.

NATE 'N AL'S DELI

The favored noshing place for many of Beverly Hills' most famous personalities has remained a solid tradition for more than 50 years with writers, producers, directors and wannabes mingling with the not-so-famous regulars, sharing their love for a good pastrami on rye.

SCOTT HUVER'S "CHEESECAKE" POSE

I met with writer Scott Huver at The Cheesecake Factory on Beverly Drive, a popular gathering place, where we enjoyed one of the best strawberry shortcakes I have ever tasted. Then we checked out the latest headlines at the newspaper vending boxes outside. Scott got his start at the *Beverly Hills Courier* where he became well known for his colorfully detailed peeks into the city's rich history. Scott has seen the city from just about every angle—from riding around in a police car at midnight to sharing cocktails with the stars at the ritziest of entertainment industry awards parties.

OPPOSITE PAGE
OBACHINE

Yet another gastronomic offering from the fertile mind of *über*-chef Wolfgang Puck and his wife, Barbara Lazaroff, ObaChine brings the tastes, smells and sights of classic Pan-Asian cuisine to Beverly Drive.

ON CAÑON DRIVE

Cañon—which takes its name from the Spanish word for *canyon* (because it descends down from Coldwater Canyon) but is usually pronounced like the weapon *cannon*—was one of the first three streets created for the city. Cañon Drive is the Beverly Hills equivalent of Main Street, a haven for independent shops and restaurants.

Carroll & Co. moved its distinctive men's clothing store from Rodeo Drive to Cañon Drive, adding a new touch of class to the street. Cañon Drive also boasts the greatest concentration of hair stylists and beauty salons in Beverly Hills, including Bruno & Soonie, Guiseppi Franco, Licari, Umberto, Valerie, Ben Simon, Aida Thibiant, Spa Thiva and more.

Cañon Drive is practically Beverly Hills' Little Italy section with a string of Italian restaurants lining the street. La Scala, Cafe Roma, Il Pastaio and Mulberry Street Pizzeria are among the current choices. There has also been a renaissance of famous-name eateries on the street: a new version of the legendary Chasen's and a fresh incarnation of Wolfgang Puck's famed Spago.

CHASEN'S
What becomes a Hollywood legend best? How about a whole new look and location, like the one here, for the legendary Tinseltown eatery Chasen's, which for years served up its famous chili, among other gastronomic delights, for every luminary and dignitary imaginable (President Ronald Reagan and his wife Nancy were devoted customers) before closing its doors in 1995. Two years later Chasen's rose phoenix-like and found a new home on Cañon Drive. The look may have changed but the style, the elegance and especially the chili remain undimmed.

ON CAÑON DRIVE

ROBERT DAVI ENJOYS A CIGAR

His face is familiar for the many "heavy" roles he plays in film—as in the James Bond film "License to Kill"—and dramatic turns on TV—as the male lead in NBC's "Profiler"—but to me actor Robert Davi's dark and intense looks merely lie at the surface of one of the most affable people I know. Together we relaxed in his favorite Beverly Hills hangout, the ultra-private Grand Havana Room where superstars and moguls, who pay thousands of dollars for private humidor lockers, enjoy the finest cigars undisturbed in a luxurious lounge atmosphere.

MULBERRY ST. PIZZERIA

Mulberry St. Pizzeria brings New York-style cuisine to Beverly Hills. It also adds a dash of Hollywood. Some lucky customers find themselves waited on by actress and part owner Cathy Moriarty and sitting next to frequent customers Billy Crystal, Danny Aiello, Matt Dillon and Joe Pesci.

THE FARMERS' MARKET PETTING ZOO

**ZYDECO BAND
AT THE FARMERS' MARKET**

< **THE FARMERS' MARKET**

A four-piece zydeco band livens up the weekly Farmers' Market, which takes over a stretch of South Cañon Drive every Sunday. The market, which features special theme weeks highlighting certain foods, sets up children's entertainment like puppet shows and petting zoos and has become a regular meeting place for people from within and outside Beverly Hills. Despite the down-home trappings, you'll still remember you're in Beverly Hills when you see stars like Melissa Etheridge looking over the wares or Spago's Wolfgang Puck judging a chili cook-off. Dozens of produce dealers set up stands with colorful canopies of high-quality fresh produce trucked in from California's Central Valley.

KIOKO

In keeping with my book's theme, Kioko's window on Cañon Drive couldn't express *amoré* any better. Kioko has been designing glamorous gowns to order for more than 20 years, and her diminutive dog—whose tremendous bark far outshines its size— greets shoppers at the door while bedecked in the latest in canine couture.

LE GRAND PASSAGE

Beverly Hills needs so much space for storefronts, it sometimes cuts right through the middle of buildings to make room for more. Le Grand Passage on Cañon Drive is modeled after the Passage de Port shopping gallery in St. Tropez and houses Caffe Roma, boutiques and beauty salons.

SEALING THE DEAL AT CAFFE ROMA >
International television and motion picture distributors Douglas and Bobbi Valentine Heller celebrate the close of an important business deal with a toast at Caffe Roma in Le Grand Passage.

A BEVERLY HILLS BICYCLE OFFICER
Beverly Hills police bicycle patrol officer Jennifer Ayre makes her rounds in the business district. The patrol has been particularly effective in fighting crime and increasing the bond between the business community and the police.

DINING AT LA SCALA
Since 1959 La Scala has been *the* place to enjoy a chopped salad enhanced with salami as well as mouth-watering cannelloni. Like many local restaurants with outdoor accommodations, La Scala caters to discriminating customers of all types—even furry ones.

THE CAÑON THEATER >
One of the few "legitimate" theaters on the Westside, the Cañon alternately hosts projects starring name talent like Charlton Heston, Jackie Mason and Lynn Redgrave and productions featuring emerging stars like the singing men of "Forever Plaid."

WOLFGANG PUCK AND BARBARA LAZAROFF AT SPAGO

Passion for excellence is the main ingredient in the spectacular new Spago Beverly Hills, the latest offspring and alchemy of the husband-wife team of restaurateurs chef Wolfgang Puck and architectural designer Barbara Lazaroff.

The Austrian-born Wolfgang captured the heart (and stomach) of the Entertainment Industry with his culinary wizardry, changing forever the way America dines. Barbara designed the unique ambiences that illuminate their ventures, all as fresh as her husband's dishes. Whether you are dining beneath the drama of the vaulted interior ceiling, surrounded by a gallery of fine art and mesmerized by the silent "danse des cuisiniers" in the exhibition kitchen or you dine al fresco enveloped by the one hundred-year old olive trees beside the romantic fountain, your senses will be awakened.

Life and passion burn brightly in this charming couple.

SOMPER FURS

Felix Presburger, who worked closely under legendary screen costume designer Edith Head is today widely considered the "dean" of fur designers. A haven of exquisite elegance on North Cañon Drive, Somper provides sumptuous furs to the Beverly Hills elite and costumes major Hollywood stars like Madonna in "Dick Tracy," Sharon Stone in "Casino," Kate Winslet in "Titanic," and the ladies of "The First Wives Club."

CARROLL & CO.
The elegant men's clothier Carroll & Co. set the standard for Beverly Hills' fashionable retail community, opening its doors on Rodeo Drive in 1953. Richard Carroll's fine merchandise drew the celebrity crowd, including Cary Grant, Fred Astaire and Gene Kelly, and helped establish Rodeo Drive as a center for fashion. The store, now run by Carroll's son John, relocated in 1996 to a site on nearby Cañon Drive that features an art deco facade, rich paneling and spacious skylight. One original detail retained was the little electric locomotive which chugged around the Rodeo Drive space for decades. It now runs along a track that circles the distinctive skylight.

THE TIME MACHINE >
The vibrant and witty Paula Kent Meehan, whose search for the perfect make-up products led her to found the Redken cosmetics empire, met me at the "castle gates" of her latest venture, the Time Machine on Cañon Drive. A true hostess, Paula envisioned this colorful playland/party place for children (and some adults!) packed with a plethora of delightful toys and fantasy environments, allowing kids' imaginations to run wild. The Time Machine is just one part of Paula's new KenQuest building, which also features a classic Japanese rooftop garden overlooking all of Beverly Hills.

TIGER ON SAFARI AT TIME MACHINE

LOOKING YOUR BEST IN BEVERLY HILLS

People of all ages, ambitions and walks of life are drawn to Beverly Hills from all over the world, and they quickly discover that Beverly Hills time is not measured at a frantic pace. There is a "laid-back" feeling here, where seeing and being seen is a way of life.

Looking your very best is the only way to go. When you know you'll be seen, why not join the parade of beautiful people who work hard at being beautiful? Beverly Hills has more beauty and hair salons, spas, dermatologists and plastic surgeons within its tiny borders than any other city in the world! It's fun to look good and an adventure to find the proper hair stylist, manicurist, facialist, skin expert, and masseur or masseuse to keep you looking that way. The very ease of access to so many artistic practitioners of the beauty trade—for women *and* men—gives you a wide choice of the very best.

Cosmetic promotions are a prime activity every month with gifts and free makeovers at the department stores. These promotions are seductive, judging from what I have collected over the past year. I am running out of space to put all the new makeup, skin cleansers, eye creams, body lotions, lipsticks, eye shadows and novel beauty aid products. Perfume is also a top item, so when in the stores follow the lady with the scent you love, and perhaps you'll find the perfect perfume your special *someone* can't resist.

Men, too, are no slouches when it comes to their appearance. Toiletries, hair care and skin products are big business here. Gyms can keep you in shape physically, but it is the masters of illusion —the hair stylists, the clothiers, the masseurs—who deserve the real credit.

You can spot the natives of Beverly Hills by their fresh, healthy look and a passion for looking their best at any age.

CHRISTOPHE
The always-in-demand stylist best known for once trimming President Clinton's locks on Air Force One, working his magic on my friend Franzisca de George's hair.

THE LASKY CLINIC

One must *always* look their best in Beverly Hills, and where nature may have been initially uncooperative, the Lasky Clinic stands ready to assist you in putting your best face (or whatever) forward, specializing in all varieties of plastic surgery, cosmetic dermatology and reconstructive surgery.

JOSÉ EBER SALON

José Eber, who you might know best from his famous hair care products or many makeovers on the Oprah Winfrey show, does indeed style tresses on the premises of his luxurious 2 Rodeo salon and spa.

THE BUSINESS OF BEAUTY AT UMBERTO

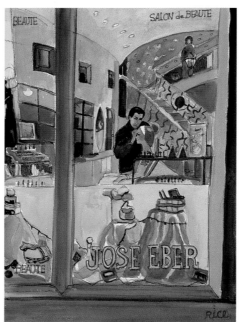

WORKING OUT, BEVERLY HILLS STYLE >

KC Winkler and Chris Kahn, two of the area's foremost fitness professionals and proud owners of some very buffed bodies, work up a sweat within Lesley Goldberg's At Your Side, a personal training studio located in Beverly Hills' Industrial Area at which they help sculpt their clients into modern day versions of Venus and Adonis.

ON "LITTLE" SANTA MONICA BOULEVARD

Don't let the diminutive name fool you. When South Santa Monica Boulevard—or "Little" Santa Monica as it is more commonly known—enters Beverly Hills it becomes part of one of the most vital business districts in the world.

Going east, the street whisks you past such Beverly Hills staples like The Musuem of Television and Radio, Jimmy's Restaurant, the Friar's Club, the Beverly Hills Family Y, and the Peninsula Hotel.

When it crosses Wilshire Boulevard next to the swooping surface of the Creative Artists Agency, it leads you directly to the heart of the shopping district, meeting up with, among other streets, Rodeo Drive. Little Santa Monica has its own distinctive features: the gorgeous Crustacean restaurant, The Sharper Image, The Players Restaurant, The Wine Merchant, Johnny Rocket's, Baja Fresh Cantina, Radio Shack, the historic Writers and Artists Building and more, from bank edifices to small, select boutiques, restaurants and specialty shops. By the time you pass the "futuristic" Union 76 Station and the glorious Western Atlas headquarters where Little Santa Monica suddenly becomes Burton Way, you'll know there's nothing small-time about it.

WESTERN ATLAS HEADQUARTERS
One of the most stunning sights in all of Beverly Hills is the classically beautiful Western Atlas Building (once known as the Litton Building), a magnificent Georgian-style structure designed by prominent architect Paul R. Williams in 1937. Situated between two black iron gates at the southeast corner of Little Santa Monica Boulevard and Crescent Drive, fountains and pools lead up to the building which features pillars taken from actress Marion Davies' famous Santa Monica beach house. At the east end are formal gardens ideal for a peaceful stroll.

GAS STATION ON CRESCENT
A streamlined, ultra-mod (in its day) hyperbolic parabola design by William Pereira and Charles Luckman highlights the Union 76 Station at the southwest corner of Little Santa Monica Boulevard and Crescent Drive.

HOLIDAY DECORATIONS AT THE ENTRANCE TO THE OVERSTREET BUILDING

HAMILTONS AND OVERSTREET'S
When actor George Hamilton isn't in front of
the cameras or soaking up the sun, he dreams
up business ventures like this chic wine bar and
cigar lounge alongside The Wine Merchant on
Little Santa Monica Boulevard. The eternally
handsome Hamilton has been a Beverly Hills
mainstay since his early days in Hollywood.

THE SHARPER IMAGE

One of the best grown-up "toy stores" in Beverly Hills, this shop offers everything the over-stressed exec could hope for, from battery-operated massage devices to soothing lava lamps to the latest in micro-stereo technology. And for those bitten by the collector's bug, look for specialty items like the $5,000 life-size statue of "Star Wars'" Darth Vader, complete with blinking chest panel.

CRUSTACEAN >

One of the recent additions to the international cuisine of Beverly Hills is this elegant French Colonial Asian eatery on Little Santa Monica Boulevard; the vision of San Francisco-based restaurateurs, Elizabeth An and her mother, Helene, descended from Vietnamese royalty. The structure is designed to evoke the feeling of 1930s-era Indochina and even includes an eye-catching stream that winds through the restaurant—actually a glass-covered 6,000 gallon serpentine aquarium sunk three feet into the floor and filled with gorgeously vibrant koi. The exotic special effect makes you feel as though you are walking on water. Guests like Harrison Ford, Warren Beatty, Annette Bening, Danny DeVito, Tori Spelling, Eddie Murphy, Larry King, Oliver Stone and Nancy Reagan have made the dining room look like a Who's Who of Hollywood celebrities.

THE BEVERLY HILLS
SHIELD AND SISTER CITY SIGN
The signpost beside the shield at the city limits outside the Little Santa Monica headquarters of Arista Records (home to top artists like Sarah McLachlan) salutes Beverly Hills' "Sister City" Cannes, France—site of the legendary annual international film festival. Each year the two cities engage in social and cultural exchanges.

THE PENINSULA HOTEL
Nestled amid the numerous service shops and restaurants that line Little Santa Monica Boulevard you can find a stunning oasis of European charm in the Peninsula Beverly Hills, a French Renaissance-style hotel, and the only Mobil Travel Guide Five-Star and AAA Five-Diamond hotel in Beverly Hills.

Need a translator to explain some of the finer points of your international deal? The Peninsula will provide one. Want a Swedish massage or some aroma body therapy? The Peninsula Spa has both. Want to dine under the stars? Try the Roof Garden patio for romantic ambience. Want to rub elbows *with* the stars? The swanky Peninsula Bar continually hosts some of the entertainment industry's most famous faces, who sip martinis an arm's length away.

TEA IN THE PENINSULA HOTEL
I especially enjoy the impeccable
High Tea in The Living Room.

THE FRIARS CLUB >
The venerable Friars Club, the legendary
hangout where hundreds of the sharpest wits in
Hollywood have traded affectionate barbs while
enjoying each other's company, was founded in
1946 by Milton Berle, Jack Benny and George
Burns in the tradition of the New York original
(and because they needed a place to play cards).
In 1996 the Friars Club celebrated its 50th
anniversary by adding a high-tech health club
with a sauna and steam room and a revamped
dining room ready for "roasting." The
membership includes younger stars like
Schwarzenegger and Stallone, and ladies like
first-ever female member, attorney Gloria Allred.

THE POOL AT THE PENINSULA >
The Peninsula Hotel brings you even closer to
the sun-drenched skies of Beverly Hills with its
beautifully landscaped 60-foot rooftop lap
pool, where you can swim to your heart's
content while enjoying breathtaking views of
Beverly Hills and Century City.

HOTEL DEL FLORES
Established in 1926, this funky hotel is one of the oldest in Beverly Hills. Situated in a low-profile spot on North Crescent Drive within walking distance of the Golden Triangle, the Hotel Del Flores treats guests to its Bohemian charms.

THE PLAYERS RESTAURANT
This wooden constable welcomes diners to the long-standing restaurant The Players, which offers a cozy, intimate atmosphere and a scenic view of bustling Little Santa Monica Boulevard while dining.

DINING WITH A PINK BUNNY AT JIMMY'S
Celebrities crowd this up-scale restaurant. Owner Jimmy Murphy loves holidays, and during Halloween I dined with actress Annie McAuley (dressed as a pink bunny) and director/writer Eric Weston. Elegantly costumed and masked patrons filled the restaurant and danced the evening away.

On Camden, Bedford, Roxbury, Brighton
and the Rest

Just west of "chi-chi" Rodeo Drive, the character of the Golden Triangle alters appreciably. Although the hustle and bustle of Beverly Hills is slowed by only a pace or two, the "village" ambience of the city comes more clearly into focus on the streets near the vertex of the Triangle at the intersection of Wilshire and Santa Monica Boulevards: Camden Drive, Bedford Drive, Roxbury Drive and Brighton Way. These streets help form the fabric of a real city, boasting numerous smaller-scale retail shops, cafes, boutiques, and offices, plus a strong concentration of medical professionals of every type. Beverly Hills' tradition of excellent food is carried on with diverse dining options like The Mandarin, Prego, 456, Mr. Chow and the Brighton Coffee Shop. Emporio Armani is just around the corner on Brighton Way, adding a distinct touch of Beverly Hills glamour.

PREGO
A popular and upbeat Italian restaurant for Beverly Hills regulars on Camden Drive. The creators of Prego traveled to Italy in search of the best authentic recipes for their eatery.

< MR. CHOW
This stark black and white interior adorned with contemporary art is the cool setting for Mr. Chow's "designer" Chinese food. A favorite in-place for many Hollywood stars.

ERIC BRAEDEN AT EMPORIO ARMANI
Eric Braeden, who has starred as the dashing Victor Newman on the daytime soap opera "The Young and the Restless" since 1980, and his wife, Dale, an interior designer, stop in at Emporio Armani to check out the famed designer's fashions. Eric, who I knew back when he was starring in the sci-fi classic film "Colossus: The Forbin Project," is as charming and suave as his television alter ego, traits that have earned him the only People's Choice Award given to a daytime actor and four Daytime Emmy nominations.

CHRISTIE'S

The new Camden Drive headquarters of the famed auction house Christie's, supervised by Marcia Hobbs, was packed with collectors—including Martin Barab, Gloria Strook, Peter Spirer, Kelly Bevan-Spirer, Elizabeth An, Errol Rappaport and Connie Martinson—interested in prized tokens of Hollywood's Golden Era. The catalogue included a chair from "The Maltese Falcon," a curve-hugging dress worn by Marilyn Monroe in "How to Marry a Millionaire" and a signature gold "TCB" lightning flash pendant given by Elvis Presley to his father, Vernon. The centerpiece of the sale included items from the estate of Claudette Colbert.

LUNCH IN THE SUN

On a beautiful day on Bedford Drive, cookbook author Eleanor Sloan and I people-watched and took in all the street's lunchtime activity.

THE MANDARIN
A gathering of businessmen at The Mandarin Chinese restaurant, no doubt forging an ambitious corporate strategy.

BRIGHTON COFFEE SHOP
One of the most popular hangouts for locals, the Brighton Coffee Shop is the oldest existing coffeehouse/luncheonette in Beverly Hills.

RESTAURANT 456
George Skorka and Egon Naday are partnered in this tiny epicurean haven tucked away at 456 North Bedford Drive. The delicious menu can best be described as Continental-Fusion.

ON SOUTH BEVERLY DRIVE

The side of Beverly Drive south of Wilshire Boulevard offers a glimpse into Beverly Hills' small town roots, for it still maintains a homey feel with independent shops that offer everything from specialty bikinis to magazines and newspapers to photo development, as well as a variety of both upscale and quick-stop dining options like Islands, California Pizza Kitchen, Koo Koo Roo, Rosti, The Coffee Bean and Tea Leaf, Hamburger Hamlet and Ruth's Chris Steak House. Amid these more down-to-earth operations you can also find the Beverly Hills Chamber of Commerce and Visitor's Bureau, which strives to promote the local Noah's Bagels as assiduously as Armani.

One is tempted to think of this side of the street as the "normal" section of Beverly Hills, until over lunch one realizes just how many gorgeous-looking young people are strolling and dining nearby—thanks to a small pocket of modeling agencies located on the street.

FOUR CORNERS AT CHARLEVILLE
Silent film star Corinne Griffith was more than just a pretty face. She also had a shrewd head for business, one which she combined with her fervent love of Beverly Hills when she dreamed up a plan for the identical New Orleans-style "Four Corners" properties which stand—one building at each corner—at the intersection of South Beverly Drive and Charleville Boulevard. Today the buildings, such as "Corner #2" here, are filled with small specialty shops and restaurants like California Pizza Kitchen, the Joy Store, and Kaché Beauty Salon, where I get my hair done.

CHEZ GILLES

Through a green leaf and flower trellis you enter a
brick patio to dine in a quiet, romantic French
restaurant on South Beverly Drive. Chef Gilles Epié, who
revitalized L'Orangerie in West Hollywood and is known
for his Miravile in Paris, has transformed the intimate
eatery—designed like a country stone cottage with two
dining rooms and an open air courtyard—and serves up
some of the best *terrine de foie gras* on the West Coast.

126

DAVID LEVI'S

Beverly Hills is a haven for collectors with more-than-modest budgets for their manias. Specialty shops like David's Levi's on South Beverly Drive—catering to the kid in everyone—are dotted throughout the city.

THE COFFEE BEAN AND TEA LEAF

No place quenches the afternoon thirsts of Beverly Hills residents quite like The Coffee Bean and Tea Leaf. In fact, the place has proven so popular as a local hangout it has not one but two outlets in the business district on Beverly Drive—one to the north of Wilshire Boulevard and this one to the south.

127

LIFE SOUTH OF WILSHIRE

The homes here are more modest and the walls and fences aren't as high, giving this section of Beverly Hills a comfortable "neighborhood" feel, full of life and vitality, which is accentuated by the schools, parks and community activity that characterize the area.

GATE OF HOME ON SOUTH RODEO

HOUSE OF ROSES

ROOFTOPS

One of my favorite sights in Beverly Hills is located on South Roxbury Drive across from Roxbury Memorial Park. It is a two-story glass-enclosed penthouse designed by famed California architect Frank Gehry, which I painted from a friend's patio. Perched above a five-story apartment building, this dramatic penthouse would be an artist's dream-come-true for an art studio.

OPPOSITE TOP
LAWN BOWLERS AT ROXBURY PARK

Founded in 1927, The Beverly Hills Lawn Bowling Club is noted for its many champion players and tournaments. Its roster has included many well known citizens of Los Angeles, like Walt Disney for whom an annual tournament has been named. Wearing whites is a must for bowlers.

OPPOSITE MIDDLE
BEVERLY HILLS HIGH SCHOOL

Aside from the dreamy-teen hype resulting from the popular Fox television series "Beverly Hills 90210," Beverly Hills High School is best known for offering a first-rate public education on a par with many of the area's top private schools, and its reputation for educational excellence lures countless families to the city. I lived nearby and walked to Beverly Hills High

School, attending several worthwhile adult classes during the evening sessions (art classes, Spanish and French language classes, and Russian and Chinese history classes). I also enrolled in a "Stop Smoking" class that actually worked! The people I met in those sessions remain my friends today.

The high school, whose actual zip code is 90212, was constructed in 1927 in classic French Normandy style. Many celebrities have attended and graduated from the school, including Richard Dreyfus, Nicholas Cage, Matthew Perry, Rob Reiner, Albert Brooks, Joely Fisher, Richard Chamberlain, Nicolette Sheridan, David Schwimmer, Jonathan Silverman and Andre Previn. And, of course, the children of many celebrities, moguls and community leaders attend today.

APARTMENTS ON CHARLEVILLE
While the north end of town is characterized by extravagant mansions and lavish estates, and the south end features more down-to-earth, family-style homes, there is also no shortage of very comfortable apartment buildings and condominiums available throughout the central part of Beverly Hills.

HAWTHORNE SCHOOL
Hawthorne School's roots go all the way back to 1915 when, as the Beverly Hills Grammar School, it was erected as the first permanent educational facility in the city. Today it serves much of the tony north end of town.

A PATRIOTIC ENSEMBLE
This star-spangled young beauty took home one of the top prizes for the most patriotic outfit during city-sponsored Fourth of July festivities at Roxbury Memorial Park.

PLAYTIME IN ROXBURY MEMORIAL PARK >
I met a six-year-old girl named Gina who posed for me in Roxbury Park, and it was through her eyes that I was inspired to create my first series of paintings. Since then, the park has been redesigned and renamed Roxbury Memorial Park. Filled with beautiful trees and foliage, the park has become a Mecca for lawn bowlers, croquet players, tennis players, basketball players, little league baseball and joggers. Picnic grounds and children's playgrounds are scattered throughout the park. A community within a community, there is a clubhouse where senior adult classes and meetings are held as well as where chess and checker games take place.

WIZARD EXPRESS AT ROXBURY PARK

BASEBALL AT ROXBURY PARK
Behind the glamorous facade, Beverly Hills is also a small
town community with families and children who enjoy
all of the usual pastimes, including a Little League
program. Thanks to the city's substantial international
population, soccer is even more popular than baseball.

< IRANIAN CELEBRATION AT BEVERLY HILLS HIGH
Beverly Hills is home to a substantial Persian/Iranian
population which is an integral part of the city. Functions
such as the Now Ruz Iranian New Year celebration at the
high school athletic field have become must-attend
events for locals from every culture.
Towering above the party, against the gleaming
backdrop of skyrises in neighboring Century City, is
the high school's very own oil well, which pumps
"black gold" from beneath the campus and provides
added revenue for the school district's budget.

LIFE SOUTH OF SUNSET

Although the homes south of Sunset Boulevard aren't emphasized by the magnificence of the lush Hills of Beverly like their counterparts north of Sunset are, they are every bit as grand and stunning. Twisting, palm-lined streets with spectacular home after spectacular home creates one of the most visually resplendent neighborhoods in America.

O'NEILL HOUSE
Located on North Rodeo Drive above Santa Monica Boulevard, the main house built in 1986 was designed by Don Ramos and stands as a prime example of Gaudiesque art nouveau architecture. Each of the six craftsmen signed their names in their mosaic tile work.

THE JACARANDAS
Each spring many of the residential streets in Beverly Hills explode in lavender when the jacaranda trees that line them come into bloom. The colorful blossoms provide an air of festivity and gaiety to the city.

EL RODEO SCHOOL

Recess fills the grounds of the El Rodeo School at Whittier Drive and Wilshire Boulevard with the kinds of joyful antics and activities that have been going on there since the school opened in 1927. Nestled against the comforting greens and greenery of the Los Angeles Country Club, El Rodeo is adding state-of-the art technological innovations to keep the next generation of Beverly Hills students on the cutting edge of education.

RAPUNZEL

I spied this statue of Rapunzel letting her hair down from the "window" of a stylish home just off Rodeo Drive so, as the legend goes, her lover could scale the walls, using her locks, to join her.

< JOGGING PAST THE PALMS
Anne White, a former All-American athlete at USC, professional tennis player throughout the 1980s and a U.S. Wimbledon competitor, makes her daily jog through Beverly Hills. She begins her trek at Doheny Drive and Santa Monica Boulevard, always runs the distance of the jogging track and makes sure to include scenic, tree-lined Beverly and Maple Drives on her trip.

A PATRIOTIC HOME
An American flag flutters proudly at this cozy estate south of Sunset Boulevard.

MYSTERY MANSION

Writer William Link—best known for such classic television murder-mystery hits as "Columbo" and "Murder She Wrote"—and his actress wife, Marjorie Nelson, look cozy on the patio of their Mediterranean-style home on Elm Drive. The home took on a more sinister and shadowy air in 1989 when its living room became the site of the shotgun slayings of LIVE Entertainment executive Jose Menendez and his wife, Kitty, at the hands of their sons, Lyle and Erik. The infamy didn't faze later buyer Bill Link, who has built a career on fictional homicides. As he told me, "It's a perfect home to inspire my mystery writing."

BUGSY'S LAST STAND

In the late 1940s Rudolph Valentino's manager, Juan Romero, rented this lovely Spanish-Moorish home on Linden Drive to a prominent Beverly Hills party girl named Virginia Hill—who just happened to be the mistress of dapper mobster Benjamin "Bugsy" Siegel, who had appropriated her nickname to christen his crazy dream, the Flamingo Hotel in Las Vegas.

Bugsy, who traveled in celebrity circles that included his boyhood pal George Raft and actor Cary Grant, also appropriated much of the Mob's financing for the hotel and casino to line his own pockets. Thus, on a June night in 1947, nine shots shattered one of the home's picture windows (Virginia was wisely in Europe at the time) and left the Bug in a dead heap on her chintz couch. The actual identity of his killer(s) remains an unsolved mystery to this day.

LUPE VELEZ'S HACIENDA >

The diminutive 40s-era actress known as the Mexican Spitfire was infamous for her furious temper and unabashedly public rows with lovers like Gary Cooper and husband, Johnny Weissmuller. Her rocky road to celebrity ended in 1944 in this Rodeo Drive hacienda when, broken-hearted after yet another ill-fated affair, the 36-year-old actress painstakingly made herself as beautiful as possible, reclined in her bed in a slinky nightgown and swallowed a bottle of sleeping pills, dreaming how ravishing she would look in death the next day.

Fate had another idea in mind for poor Lupe. According to legend, the pills reacted badly with her spicy last meal and provoked a mad dash toward the bathroom. She tripped and pitched forward head-first into the commode, where she was discovered dead the following morning.

THE EAST END

The action in Beverly Hills doesn't stop with the attractions of the city's Golden Triangle or its jaw-dropping estates. The east side of the city has its own particular flavor.

La Cienega Boulevard, which is home to the Academy of Motion Picture Arts and Science's Center for Motion Picture Study, the always busy Tennis Center and the popular La Cienega Park, forms a buffer between Beverly Hills and its neighbor, Los Angeles. It is in Beverly Hills that the famed La Cienega-based "Restaurant Row" begins in earnest, serving as home to such favorite eateries as Lawry's The Prime Rib, the Stinking Rose, Gaylord's of India, Benihana of Tokyo, Ed Debevic's and the Beverly Hills Cafe.

At the eastern border is the city's "Industrial Area" which, despite its name, hosts its own high-end businesses like Maple Drive Restaurant, Playboy Enterprises, the Hilton Hotels Corporation and Beverly Hills Ltd. Mercedes-Benz. The Maple Counseling Center, known for its tireless efforts offering psychiatric counseling and substance abuse programs, is another plus.

Another east side street is Robertson Boulevard, which boasts glamour designer Nolan Miller's couturier studio, the Beverly Hills Playhouse, the sidewalk cafe Paddington's and the Beverly Hills Martial Arts Center.

The Academy of Motion Picture Arts and Sciences anchors the east end of Wilshire Boulevard, and the area is bolstered by major entertainment firms like International Creative Management.

QUIET ON THE SET!
I came across this location shoot—one of the many motion picture, television and commercial shoots staged in Beverly Hills—while painting near the baseball diamond in La Cienega Park one day.

NOLAN MILLER OUTFITS JACKIE COLLINS

From his Robertson Boulevard salon, famed fashion designer Nolan Miller—whose lavish creations practically define Hollywood glamour and elegance—begins work on a new creation sure to suit novelist Jackie Collins, one of his most devoted admirers, to a tee. Miller rocketed to the top with his design work for television, particularly his collaborations with superproducer Aaron Spelling ("Dynasty," "The Love Boat").

Off-screen he has dressed top stars including Ann-Margret, Sophia Loren, Elizabeth Taylor, Barbra Streisand, Whoopi Goldberg and Heather Locklear on her wedding day. Jackie Collins is also well-versed in the ways of the rich and famous, having written 17 steamy bestsellers ("Hollywood Wives," "Lucky") that often chronicle life, love and intrigue within the mansions of her current hometown, Beverly Hills.

MORTON'S
One of the epicenters of Hollywood power dining, located on the border of Beverly Hills. Monday nights offer the best chance to glimpse Hollywood royalty, with a clientele ranging from Michael Douglas to Nicole Kidman. The annual Oscar night party thrown there by *Vanity Fair* magazine is considered one of the hottest soirées of the season.

BEVERLY HILLS LTD. MERCEDES-BENZ SHOWROOM
If these classic antique models aren't what you had in mind, Beverly Hills Ltd. Mercedes-Benz has an entire showroom of newer models for your consideration. Beverly Hills is a city of car lovers. The streets have seen almost every kind of auto, from Elvis' Maserati to Angelyne's pink Corvette to the original 1960s Batmobile designed by George Barris.

EARLY MODEL T FORD

LATE 1930s PACKARD CONVERTIBLE

BEVERLY HILLS ANIMAL HOSPITAL
Veterinarians located in the cozy corner of
the city known as the Industrial Area tend to
the ills of some of the most pampered pets on
the planet, as animal lovers in Beverly Hills
spare no expense. The pet doctors here
sometimes need a broader area of expertise
than canine and feline anatomy, however; some
of the more unusual companions the city has
seen include an ocelot named "Baby," various
pythons and boa constrictors, chattering
monkeys and strutting peacocks. Police once
ticketed a man for walking his full-grown
Bengal tiger around town on a leash!

**SCULPTURE DESIGN IMPORTS
ON ROBERTSON**
Perched on pedestals, these hand-carved Greek
and Roman impostors hewn of imposing Italian
Carrara marble, along with their terra cotta
brethren, grace the gated grounds of many
Beverly Hills homes. Culture comes at a price—
usually five figures.

TEMPLE EMMANUEL CHAPEL
The children of Temple Emmanuel Nursery School celebrate
Shabbat in the Harrison Chapel with joyous songs balanced
with reverent prayer led by program director Alicia Magal
and Cantor Edward Krawel. The only Reform Temple in the
city, it was built in 1954. The Temple is rich with cultural and
religious heritage, such as the images on the wall seen here—
symbols dating back to the Third Century in Galilee, Israel.

THE BEVERLY HILLS TENNIS CLUB
The well-known motion picture attorney Louis Blau invited me to visit the Beverly Hills Tennis Club, which was established in 1929. It soon became as much of a Hollywood hangout as it was a place to perfect your backhand (young Jimmy Connors trained here), with the membership over the years including such bygone players as Cary Grant, Ginger Rogers, John Huston, Barbara Stanwyk, the Marx Brothers, Doris Day, Laurence Olivier, Charlie Chaplin, Paulette Goddard and Gilbert Roland. Today the ranks have expanded to include up-and-coming movie makers, doctors, lawyers and other young professionals. While enjoying a terrific lunch on the patio, I watched players enjoy the championship-level courts.

ROB AND JULIE MORAN AT MAPLE DRIVE

I enjoyed happy hour at Maple Drive, Tony Bill's fabulous out-of-the-way restaurant that boasts investors Liza Minelli and Dudley Moore and traditionally hosts the Elton John AIDS Foundation's annual Oscar night bash. My companions were one of Hollywood's emerging "power couples," Rob and Julie Moran. The darkly handsome Rob has found success as an actor in such films as "Kingpin," while the effervescent Julie brings all the news from Hollywood into homes across the country every day as co-host of "Entertainment Tonight."

FINNEY'S IN THE ALLEY

Reading the latest edition of *The Beverly Hills Courier* has become a Friday tradition at Finney's in the Alley, a lunch window specializing in Philly steak sandwiches that is tucked away in an alley behind *The Courier's* offices. *The Courier* was founded in 1965 by publisher March Schwartz and his late wife, Wendy Lee, as a weekly journal. Other long-running local publications include Seth Baker's style-minded *Beverly Hills 213* and LaVetta Forbes' high society magazine *Beverly Hills 90212*, the oldest minority-owned business in the city; the three of them bringing you all the news from the biggest "small town" in the world.

BEVERLY HILLS MARTIAL ARTS CENTER
A group of children get a kick out of their training at the Beverly Hills Martial Arts Center on Robertson Boulevard. Headed by Grand Master Bong C. Kim, the first U.S. World Champion in TaeKwanDo, the center trains students in a variety of disciplines, including HapKiDo, Ju'Do and TaeKwanDo. The students range in age from small children to their parents.

TRATTORIA AMICI
One of the city's best kept secrets is Trattoria Amici, tucked behind a modest hotel at the border of Beverly Hills and West Hollywood. Run by Tancredi DeLuca, the cozy Italian restaurant offers an intimate dining experience and occasional glimpses of hot young stars, like the cast of TV's "Friends," and rocker Rod Stewart.

THE HOTEL NIKKO AT BEVERLY HILLS >
Modern architecture meets Asian tradition at the stunning Hotel Nikko in Los Angeles, just at the border of Beverly Hills. The hotel is perfectly suited for business or pleasure and features a breathtaking zen garden.

152

LA PROMENADE AT THE FOUR SEASONS
These romantic statues liven up the entrance of
the fabulous Four Seasons Hotel, which lies just
one block outside of Beverly Hills in Los Angeles.

LAWRY'S THE PRIME RIB

When you're ready to forget California cuisine and want to indulge your more carnivorous appetites, Lawry's The Prime Rib on Restaurant Row is the place to be in Beverly Hills. As my artist friend Lois Rich and I discovered, the roast beef doesn't come thicker, juicier or more tender anywhere else.

THE PAINTER AT THE FOUR SEASONS

No, I didn't catch a workman in the act of sprucing up the Four Seasons Hotel. This eye-catching statue, one of my favorites, adds a sprightly charm to the elegant hostelry.

THE ENTERTAINMENT INDUSTRY

When the geographical area known as Hollywood became synonymous in the national consciousness with fast-living, rule-breaking movie stars indulging in forbidden pleasures in the earliest days of the century, it wasn't long before those in the film colony who fancied themselves as more "respectable" began migrating to newly posh Beverly Hills.

Douglas Fairbanks led the charge in 1919 when he needed a very private love nest to carry on his affair with Mary Pickford (both were still married at the time) and discovered a rustic hunting cabin that he remodeled into the prototype for all movie star homes, Pickfair. Famous faces like Gloria Swanson, Charlie Chaplin, Tom Mix, Ronald Colman, Carl Laemmle, John Barrymore, Buster Keaton, Harold Lloyd, Jack Warner, Clara Bow, Marion Davies and Rudolph Valentino soon followed suit. Thus was born Beverly Hills' still-enduring—and still-true—reputation as a choice address for the stars. Today, Bruce Springsteen, Jay Leno, Jack Lemmon, Frank Sinatra, Candice Bergen, Steve Martin, Mary Hart, Jacqueline Bissett and Jeffrey Katzenberg are just a few of the names in "the Industry" who call the city their home.

Led by the prestigious Academy of Motion Picture Arts and Sciences, over 500 entertainment-related industries are located in Beverly Hills, ranging from talent brokers like the William Morris Agency, Creative Artists Agency, United Talent Agency and International Creative Management, to DreamWorks Records to Polygram Filmed Entertainment to BMG to Castle Rock to Gramercy Pictures to Virgin Records to Dove Books. Of course, it doesn't hurt that many of these companies' top executives can drive five minutes to work, or even *walk* in some cases.

Hollywood the Dream lives on in Beverly Hills.

CELLULOID STATUE
The history of Beverly Hills has always been intermingled with that of some of the greatest stars in Hollywood, and their legacy is commemorated in "Celluloid," a 15-foot statue on the traffic island at the intersection of Olympic Boulevard, Beverly Drive and Beverwil Drive. The piece—featuring bas relief images of Charlie Chaplin, Douglas Fairbanks, Mary Pickford, Harold Lloyd, Will Rogers, Tom Mix, Rudolph Valentino, Conrad Nagel and Fred Niblo—was constructed in 1959 by sculptor Merrell Gage. Their efforts are remembered, with this inscription:

"In tribute to those celebrities of the motion picture industry who worked so valiantly for the preservation of Beverly Hills as a separate municipality."

TIN MAN, SCARECROW, COWARDLY LION

THE CENTER FOR MOTION PICTURE STUDY >
This Spanish Colonial Revival-style building on La Cienega Boulevard served faithfully as the city's waterworks until the local government and the Academy of Motion Picture Arts and Sciences entered into an agreement to convert it into a climate-controlled repository for the Academy's vast Margaret Herrick Library of historical archives, as well as film and photo still collections.

I was present at the elaborate party on January 23, 1991 when the film industry and its many stars celebrated the opening of the Center and honored fund-raisers Bob Hope, Meryl Streep, Michael Douglas, the Mary Pickford Foundation and the Cecil B. De Mille Trust. It since has become the mecca for film scholars and historians from around the world.

THE ACADEMY OF MOTION PICTURE ARTS AND SCIENCES

Of all Beverly Hills' bonds to the entertainment industry, none is more prestigious than its role as home for the headquarters of the seven-decade-old Academy, which has been lodged in a black Maxwell Starkman-designed structure on Wilshire Boulevard for more than 20 years.

Although the Academy is best known for its annual, highly-hyped and much coveted Oscar awards ceremonies which I enjoy attending, and the eyes of the world turn to Beverly Hills in the wee hours of the morning each February for the live announcement of the year's nominees in the 1,111-seat state-of-the-art Samuel Goldwyn Theater, the organization is also involved in film history, preservation and restoration projects—all funded by the television advertising income from that one grand evening of celebrating the best Hollywood has to offer. "Casablanca" screenwriter Julius Epstein and his wife, Ann, and actors Henry Silva and Bert Williams are among those descending the sweeping staircase of the Academy Theater.

"THE SLUMS OF BEVERLY HILLS"

"The Slums of Beverly Hills" does not, of course, refer to any real area in the city— there is no undesirable section. Rather, it is the title of a Fox Searchlight Pictures film written and directed by Tamara Jenkins that I caught shooting in the shadow of the Civic Center one day. Produced by Robert Redford, the movie boasts a cast of both newcomers and veterans that includes Alan Arkin, Natasha Lyonne, Marisa Tomei, Carl Reiner, Kevin Corrigan, Rita Moreno and Polly Bergen.

STEVE MARTIN'S HOME

The sleek modern exterior reflects the refined taste of the well-known actor, writer and comedian, who is also an avid enthusiast of fine art. Martin affectionately skewered many of the aspects of the Beverly Hills lifestyle in his self-penned celluloid valentine, "L.A. Story."

CREATIVE ARTISTS AGENCY

The art of the deal is practiced and frequently perfected on a daily basis within the walls of this widely-hailed design masterpiece executed by I.M. Pei for the Creative Artists Agency, one of the most powerful entities in Hollywood. Built into a star-making giant and headed by Mike Ovitz throughout the 1980s and mid-1990s, CAA established itself as a celebrity in its own right by representing an ever-expanding roster of some of the biggest names in the entertainment industry, including Kevin Costner, Whitney Houston, David Letterman and Robert Redford.

Poised at one of the city's most prestigious gateways—the intersection of Santa Monica and Wilshire Boulevards—CAA shows off the fruits of art and commerce with the overwhelming Roy Lichtenstein original painting "Bahais" that dominates the skylighted lobby.

SCARLETT O'HARA DOLL

WRITERS GUILD THEATER

The Writers Guild Theater on Doheny Drive is one of the best private places in Beverly Hills for members of the Guild to meet, greet and preview a new film. The 540-seat theater recently underwent an extensive revamp and now features amenities like Crestron Crestlite digital lighting, Marquee chairs for total body support, state-of-the-art sound equipment installed for a variety of top systems, and top quality projection.

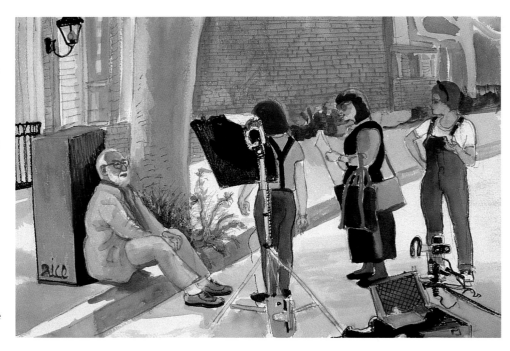

SAUL ZAENTZ'S PHOTO OP

The legendary independent film producer Saul Zaentz, whose credits include the Oscar-winning "One Flew Over the Cuckoo's Nest" and "Amadeus," is ready for his *own* close-up sitting curbside on Lasky Drive—all part of the media hoopla leading up to the 69th Annual Academy Awards in 1997, where Zaentz received the Irving Thalberg Award.

The Thalberg wasn't all he took home on Oscar night. With "The English Patient's" Best Picture win (along with eight other Oscar statuettes), Zaentz achieved the envious distinction of having produced Best Films in three separate decades.

THE FINE ARTS THEATER

Built as the Regina Wilshire Theater in 1937, this compact model of Art Deco stylings has endured a number of ownership changes and recently found new life—with some of its original features restored—as the Fine Arts Theater; it now screens dozens of avant-garde and adventurous new films.

OPPOSITE PAGE
A LUNCH DATE AT THE GRILL

Although the stunning actress Jacqueline Bisset hails from England, her successful Hollywood career—which includes the film "Scenes From the Class Struggle In Beverly Hills"—has led her to keep homes in Beverly Hills and Malibu. She told me over lunch at The Grill On the Alley that she enjoys Beverly Hills because it feels comfortable and warm, much like her friendship with well-known talent agent and raconteur extraordinaire Robert Littman. The Grill is *the* spot in Beverly Hills to catch top names like Jacqueline and Robert breaking bread; just a quick walk from some of the major talent agencies in The Biz, it serves as one of the prime deal-making sites in the city.

JIMMY STEWART'S HOME
One of the most venerable of the silver screen superstars to have graced the ranks of the citizenry of Beverly Hills, America's beloved Everyman, Jimmy Stewart, spent the last several decades of his wonderful life residing on a peaceful stretch of Roxbury Drive that looks as if it was taken straight out of "It's a Wonderful Life." Perfectly normal, except for the fact that at one time his immediate neighbors included Lucille Ball, Jack Benny and Ronald Colman.

LAEMMLE MUSIC HALL THEATER
Owned by the family of film pioneer Carl Laemmle, the 1937-era Art Deco Music Hall on Wilshire Boulevard was recently converted into a multi-screen theater and is one of the best places for cinema enthusiasts to catch the latest in independent and foreign films. In the 1950s, the Music Hall truly lived up to its name, as the home to a popular television show starring the flamboyant pianist Liberace.

THE WICKED WITCH OF THE WEST DOLL

THE WITCH'S HOUSE >
Designed by Henry Oliver in 1921 as a movie set and office for a Hollywood production company, the thatched roof Hansel and Gretel-style structure was moved intact from its original location in Culver City to its present address on Walden Drive. Known as the "Witch's House," it is now a private residence—as well as a familiar local landmark seen in films like "Clueless"—that draws both children and adults to daydream at its fence.

GARBO'S RETREAT

This enchanting English country hideaway in the flats of Beverly Hills is one of the handful of places in the city where Greta Garbo went when she wanted to be alone. Although she was often a gregarious host, she would also occasionally cut off all contact with her friends for days at a time. Some of her pals would knock at her door to no avail, never knowing if Garbo was simply ignoring them from within. She would then emerge from seclusion without a word as if nothing unusual had happened. When she sold the home, she retained the right to use the guest house whenever she pleased, and she used it even in her later years when she would occasionally slip back into Beverly Hills without fanfare.

SHIRLEY TEMPLE DOLL

HILLARD ELKINS AT HOME
Producer/manager Hillard Elkins is the picture of tranquillity sitting by the pool of his Roxbury Drive home, which was originally built for actor Lionel Barrymore. Elkins began his career as a theatrical agent for the William Morris Agency, later opening his own management company with clients such as Steve McQueen and Mel Brooks. "Richard Pryor Live In Concert" and "Alice's Restaurant" are among his movie successes. "Hilly," as his friends call him, told me what he enjoys most about his Beverly Hills home is that he can relax and read scripts by his pool, cut off from the rest of the world.

INTERNATIONAL CREATIVE MANAGEMENT
One of the top talent brokers in Tinseltown, ICM has withstood the test of time for over two decades, gathering a powerhouse client list that includes Tommy Lee Jones, Jodie Foster, Will Smith, Mel Gibson, Julia Roberts, Steve Martin, Meg Ryan and Richard Gere, among others. The agency took up residence in its Wilshire Boulevard headquarters, complete with this distinctive black granite pyramid fountain in the courtyard, in 1992.

CONNIE MARTINSON
The name of the television show is "Connie Martinson Talks Books," and when Connie—a winner of the Davenport Prize for Literature, a former editor of *The Writer Magazine* and a public affairs expert—talks, millions of viewers of the Satellite Program Network listen, especially when she's hosting such literary lions as Gore Vidal, Sidney Sheldon, Gloria Steinem and Vice President Al Gore. When I stopped by at her Beverly Hills home, Connie was interviewing Julian Okwu, author of the book "Fast Forward: Young African American Men in a Critical Age."

THE MUSEUM OF TELEVISION AND RADIO

Conceived as a West Coast sister site to the original MT&R in New York and able to reproduce its entire collection of important television and radio broadcasts from throughout the century, this innovative, eye-catching modern structure by acclaimed architect Richard Meier is at the corner of Beverly Drive and Little Santa Monica Boulevard.

The Museum is devoted to the preservation and celebration of the broadcast industry with exhibits like a display of the futuristic costumes from "Star Trek: The Next Generation" and a vast library of TV and radio shows that can be called up for instant viewing and listening.

MARILYN MONROE DOLLS

On my first visit to Beverly Hills, I remember trying on clothes in a dressing room alongside one occupied by Marilyn at Jax. We were tossing and exchanging clothes over the partition that separated us, and we both bought the same low-cut, free-skirted checkered dress, albeit in different colors. Her personality was infectious, and she was a truly warm person.

WILLIAM MORRIS AGENCY

Since its founding in 1898, the well-known William Morris Agency—the oldest existing talent agency in the world—has held a prominent place in the entertainment industry, first in New York and later in its Beverly Hills offices on El Camino Drive. The agency continues to cultivate a reputation for representing some of the top names in movies and television, including Clint Eastwood, George Clooney and Arnold Schwarzenegger. Long famous for its entry-level mail room jobs that can ultimately lead to top executive positions, the agency has also launched the careers of media giants Barry Diller and David Geffen.

BERTELSMANN MUSIC GROUP

The gleaming headquarters of Bertelsmann Music Group (BMG) lends prestige to the much-traveled intersection of Wilshire and Robertson Boulevards. The building serves as the western regional nexus for all of the international music and video company's many divisions, which include RCA Music, BMG Music, Zoo Entertainment and Private Music.

POLYGRAM FILMED ENTERTAINMENT
The movie wing of PolyGram—known for
such commercial and critical hits as "Bean,"
"Four Weddings and a Funeral" and "Dead
Man Walking"—is the owner of this sleek and
majestic Wilshire Crescent Building. The striking
black glass and white Carrera marble structure
designed by Gin Wong & Associates features
a glass rotunda lobby and a state-of-the-art
screening room.

"A NIGHT AT THE ROXBURY"
No, these cell phone-dependent wedding
guests aren't *really* Beverly Hills natives. It's
a gag from the Paramount Pictures comedy
"A Night at the Roxbury" from "Saturday
Night Live" producer Lorne Michaels and
Amy Heckerling, the writer-producer-director
behind "Clueless." Filmmakers shot this
nuptial scene at a Cañon Drive home. Lovely
Loni Anderson strolls down the aisle followed
by Will Ferrell, who co-wrote and stars in the
film with his "SNL" castmate Chris Kattan as
the bopping, club-hopping sketch characters
"the Roxbury Guys." Of course, genuine
Beverly Hills-ians would never be so rude;
they save *their* cell phone conversations for
when they're in traffic.

THE BEVERLY HILLS PLAYHOUSE

Milton Katselas, the popular acting teacher who founded the Beverly Hills Playhouse over 20 years ago, critiques a scene from "The Waltz of the Toreadors" with renowned director Gene Reynolds (co-creator of "M*A*S*H") and actors Jocelyn Jones and Allen Williams. Saturday morning classes like this one—which was well-attended by familiar faces such as Anne Archer, Doris Roberts and Jeffrey Tambor—have helped establish the playhouse on Robertson Boulevard as one of the leading workshops for established and up-and-coming actors, directors and playwrights.

STANLEY CHASE

Beverly Park
Gardens

Painting
Elizabeth An
at Crustacean
restaurant

STANLEY CHASE

FERNANDO RODRIGUEZ

STANLEY CHASE

174

ABOUT DOROTHY RICE

Beverly Hills With Love is artist/author Dorothy Rice's fourth published book, an appreciation of one of the premier cities in the world and one which has defined glamour for the rest of the globe. She masterfully crafts her stunning watercolors to capture a diverse assortment of people, places, architecture and lifestyles and provides vital background information and engaging personal observations that combine to create a joyous and vivid picture of life in Beverly Hills.

Growing up in New York City, Dorothy Rice's childhood was continually enlivened by the procession of illustrators and photographers who worked for her father's commercial art studio. Her own art training began with night classes at the Art Students League in Manhattan while attending high school.

John Rawlings, the world renowned fashion photographer for *Vogue*, "discovered" her at age 14, and *Vogue* selected her to travel to Paris where she became the top photographic model for such legendary couturiers as Dior and Balenciaga. The resulting international acclaim led her to a career as an actress, performing frequently on Broadway, off-Broadway and on television.

She moved from New York to Beverly Hills to continue her successful acting career in Hollywood. Inspired by her new surroundings, she was ultimately drawn back to her first love: painting. She could frequently be seen setting up an easel on sidewalks, streets and other byways to create on-the-spot watercolors—images that were subsequently published in her first book of paintings, *Los Angeles With Love*, an artist's-eye-view of the City of Angels.

Dorothy Rice studied at the Otis/Parsons Art Institute in Los Angeles and the Art Center College of Design in Los Angeles and Santa Monica College, as well as at the University of Guadalajara in Mexico. She adroitly works in a variety of media—oil, palette knife, watercolor and pastel—and is one of the few American artists ever to be honored with an invitation to paint a mural in Mexico, a country known for its tradition of spectacular muralists.

Her successful one-woman show of the lush oils of Mexico, *Serenata Mexicana*, at the prestigious Southwest Museum in Los Angeles was so popular it was extended for two months. Private collectors and corporations are among those who have purchased her paintings, and her work has been exhibited in the Palm Springs Museum, the National Arts Club in New York City, Madison Avenue galleries and in other venues across the United States and abroad.

Each of her books has met with critical praise and public acclaim. *Israel With Love* depicts her sojourn through that country, a project so well-received the Israeli Ambassador in Washington, D.C., honored her with a gala reception at Israel's embassy. Artwork from *Israel With Love* has since been on a three-year sponsored tour of the United States. In her third book, *Manhattan With Love*, she embarked on a journey of the heart back to the city of her youth, creating an exceptional tribute to an unparalleled city. Paintings from the Manhattan book have served as the permanent background set of ABC's daily television series "The View" hosted by Barbara Walters.

Many publications and critics have spotlighted Dorothy Rice and her signature style, including *Architectural Digest* which devoted a major article to her work, illustrating it with many of her paintings. As Ray Bradbury noted, "Dorothy Rice has fresh eyes and her own palette. Which means a talent for making the familiar unfamiliar, younger than when you last saw it."

ERIC WESTON

END OF THE TOUR